D0245071

Best Bites

saturday kitchen

Best Bites

saturday kitchen

Over 100 simple recipes from expert chefs

contents

best
ham & pork

best
poultry & game

contents

hell

Introduction
James Martin

Welcome to the second *Saturday Kitchen* cookbook. We're calling this one *Best Bites* because that's exactly what it is, a collection of the very tastiest recipes from the very best collection of chefs anywhere in the world. I always look forward to doing the show each week and despite the early start it's always fun.

The show has gone from strength to strength and I've loved working on it. It's a real pleasure to be with such an enthusiastic team of people and we all have a great time every Saturday. The studio is always full of laughter as well as the smell of bacon sarnies and fresh coffee – we do start work at 6 a.m. remember!

I really couldn't do the show without the help of the whole team and they do a brilliant job behind the scenes to make it happen. So much preparation goes into a live weekly cookery television programme and by the time you get to see each of the recipes, we've written, tested and rehearsed each and every one of them, so you can be sure they'll work at home, too.

This book is full of a wide range of recipes which can be cooked by anyone. None of them are too difficult and all of them are delicious to eat.

It's been amazing to see some of the greatest chefs in the world cooking in the studio – where else would I get to slice mushrooms for Michel Roux for his *Coquilles Saint Jacques* or see Raymond Blanc cook his *Steak maman blanc with sauté potatoes* right in front of me? We've been able to show you some brand new faces too such as Adriana Trigiani, Jason Atherton and Jun Tanaka. And it's great to welcome back some of the many friends of *Saturday Kitchen*. Tom Aikens popped in and made a delicious

Pan-fried pork belly with scallop and squid, caramalized onions and balsamic sauce, whilst Bill Granger travelled across the globe to make us his *Hoisin and plum glazed ham with lemon potato salad.* One man whose food is always a hit on *Saturday Kitchen* (especially with the cameramen) is Atul Kochhar. His *Gymkhana chicken pie* and *Country captain chicken curry* featured here are making my stomach rumble just thinking about them.

I couldn't talk about our guest chefs without a special mention for my great mates, Si and Dave – the Hairy Bikers. Their appearances on the show are always memorable, usually because I can't keep a straight face! I love cooking with them – in between all the laughs there are always great recipes and you get four of them in this book.

We've had some brilliant celebrities on the show too and their food heaven and food hell ingredients always test my culinary skills. Once I've come up with a dish inspired by each ingredient, it's then up to the viewers to choose which one I get to cook. The recipes in this book are the ones the viewers voted for, so you can try Ronnie Corbett's food heaven *Pickled French beans with mackerel, bacon and tallegio jacket potatoes* or Griff Rhys Jones's food hell *Beef stew and dumplings.* However, you may want to be careful when you try Jessica Hynes food hell of *Grilled sardines with sauce vierge* as it nearly burnt down the studio when we cooked it!

Also in the book are some of my quick recipes – they're both appetising and inspirational. I normally only get a couple of minutes to make them on a Saturday and you'll find them very simple to do at home. So I hope you enjoy my *Chicken goujons with home-made tomato ketchup* or my *Dill blinis with caviar and sour cream* as everyone else did!

Lastly I must say a big thank you to our fantastic wine experts, Olly, Susy, Susie, Peter, Jancis and Tim. Hats off to all of you! It's not easy matching wines to such a wide variety of recipes but every week they come up with some brilliant choices and travel the length and breadth of Britain to do so. They've given out so many great tips for choosing wine and we've put many of them in the book. I've really enjoyed learning from them and they certainly have introduced me to some cracking wines, most of which are very reasonably priced too. Being a Yorkshireman I love a bargain!

I really hope you enjoy the recipes and wines in the book. Do try them all at home as I guarantee you'll enjoy eating the dishes, I know I did.

I look forward to seeing you all on Saturday mornings.

Happy Cooking!

James

Best

Starters

salmon ceviche with fennel salad

Stuart Gillies

Serves 4–6

Ingredients

For the ceviche

250g (9oz) organic salmon fillet,
skinned

2 tablespoons rock salt

1 tablespoon finely diced red chillies

75ml (3fl oz) pink grapefruit juice

150ml (5fl oz) lime juice
(about 5 limes)

10g (½oz) lime zest

20g (¾oz) caster sugar

30 coriander leaves, finely chopped

For the salad

1 fennel, finely sliced (on a mandolin
if possible)

110g (4oz) baby salad leaves

Method

- Lightly sprinkle the salmon fillet with rock salt, then place in the fridge for 20 minutes.
- Remove, carefully wash off all the salt and pat dry.
- Mix the chillies, grapefruit juice, lime juice and lime zest together and add the sugar to make a dressing.
- Add the coriander at the last minute and toss to combine.
- Place the sliced fennel into iced water for 2–3 minutes, then remove and drain. Mix with the salad leaves and a little of the dressing.
- To serve, slice the salmon at a 45 degree angle, about 2–3mm thick, trimming off any excess blood line if necessary.
- Lay several slices evenly in a single layer on the serving plate.
- Spoon the remaining dressing over the salmon.
- Place the fennel salad on top and serve.

Wine expert Susie Barrie's choice

Tesco Finest Tapiwey Vineyard Sauvignon Blanc

Ceviche comes from South America, and in the spirit of getting as close to its origins as possible, I am going to head to Chile for my choice. This Tapiwey is like munching a Granny Smith apple, with the addition of lime, grapefruit and fennel flavours. The wine is also a little bit grassy and herbal, which will complement the salmon.

When buying New World sauvignon blanc, go for the most recent vintage possible because what we are looking for in this style of wine is fruitiness and freshness.

duck breast with honey and sansho pepper and mango, shiso and diakon salad

Nic Watt

Serves 4

Ingredients

For the duck

75g (3oz) honey

15g (½oz) umeboshi paste (available from specialist Japanese grocers)

½ teaspoon finely chopped fresh ginger

¼ teaspoon sansho pepper (available from specialist Japanese grocers)

¼ teaspoon mild curry powder

¼ teaspoon Chinese five-spice powder

¼ teaspoon ground ginger

4 x 175g (6oz) duck breasts

For the salad

110g (4oz) daikon radish, finely julienned

1 mango, peeled, stone removed, finely sliced

50g (2oz) lotus root, finely sliced and deep-fried until crisp (available from Asian grocers)

75g (3oz) watercress

1 punnet shiso leaves (also called perilla leaves)

1 shallot, finely sliced

juice of ½ lemon

Method

- Preheat the oven to 160°C/320°F/Gas Mark 2.
- Place the honey in a bowl along with the umeboshi paste and fresh ginger and mix well.
- Add the sansho pepper, curry and five-spice powders and the ground ginger and blend well.
- Heat a frying pan until warm, add the duck breasts, skin side down, and cook gently for 3–4 minutes to render the fat.
- Turn the breasts over and baste with the honey mixture.
- Place in the oven for 3–4 minutes until just cooked through.
- Remove, baste once more and leave to rest.
- To serve, take a small handful of daikon and roll into a ball. Repeat until there are 28 balls of daikon and arrange 7 around the edges of each plate.
- Place 2 slices of mango on top of each ball of daikon.
- Cut the duck breasts into 2–3mm slices and place 2 pieces on top of each pile of mango and daikon.
- Place a piece of lotus root to the side of each pile.
- Toss the watercress, shiso leaves, shallot and the remaining daikon with the lemon juice and place a pile in the centre of each plate.

Wine expert Olly Smith's choice

This wine is going to work with the two aspects of the dish. It will refresh against the spice of the duck and it will back up the lovely fruitiness of the salad.

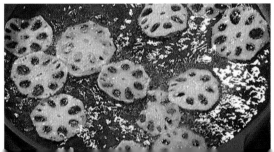

mutton, onion and mint terrine with beetroot chutney and crusty bread

James Martin

Serves 8

Ingredients

For the terrine

1 tablespoon olive oil

2 onions, finely sliced

3 tablespoons finely chopped mint

300g (11oz) streaky bacon

750g (1lb 11oz) leg of mutton, thinly sliced

salt

black pepper

For the beetroot chutney

1 tablespoon olive oil

1 red onion, finely diced

1 clove garlic, finely chopped

1 x 2cm piece of ginger, grated

1 teaspoon mustard seeds

300g (11oz) cooked beetroot

50g (2oz) caster sugar

75ml (3fl oz) sherry vinegar

salt

black pepper

To serve

1 baguette, thickly sliced

Method

- Preheat the oven to 180°C/350°F/Gas Mark 4.
- Heat a frying pan until hot and add the olive oil and onions.
- Cook for 3–4 minutes until just softened, then season with salt and black pepper and fold in the mint.
- Place to one side to cool.
- Place the bacon in a 1 litre (1 pint 15fl oz) pudding basin, lining the sides from top to bottom and leaving the bacon hanging over the top of the bowl.
- Place a little of the sliced mutton into the bottom of the bacon lined bowl, then season with salt and black pepper.
- Top with some of the onions, then repeat with alternate layers of mutton and onions until the bowl is three-quarters full.
- Flip the bacon over the filling to cover and press down.
- Cover with foil, then place in a baking tin three-quarters filled with hot water.
- Place in the oven for 2 hours, then remove and allow to cool slightly.
- Place a couple of tins on top of the cooked terrine and place in the fridge until cold.
- To prepare the chutney, heat a frying pan until hot and add the olive oil, onion, garlic and ginger.
- Cook for 2–3 minutes until just softened.
- Add the mustard seeds and cook until they pop.
- Add the beetroot, sugar and vinegar and cook for 4–5 minutes until thickened.
- Season with salt and black pepper and allow to cool.
- Cut a wedge of terrine and serve with a spoonful of chutney and a hunk of crusty bread.

vegetable and herb soup

Michael Caines

Serves 4–5

Ingredients

20g (¾oz) shallots, finely chopped

35g (1½oz) leeks, cut into 10mm dice

50g (2oz) celeriac, cut into 10mm dice

50g (2oz) carrots, cut into 10mm dice

150g (5oz) unsalted butter

50ml (2fl oz) white wine

500ml (18fl oz) water

500ml (18fl oz) chicken stock

50g (2oz) courgette, cut into
10mm dice

50g (2oz) French beans, cut into
10mm lengths

50g (2oz) fresh peas

50g (2oz) Savoy cabbage, cut into
10mm dice

110g (4fl oz) double cream

50g (2oz) tomatoes, blanched,
seeded and cut into 10mm dice

12 basil leaves, roughly chopped

5g (¼oz) sorrel, roughly chopped

5g (¼oz) chervil, roughly chopped

5g (¼oz) chives, chopped

caster sugar

salt

pepper

Method

- Sweat the shallots, leeks, celeriac and carrot with 25g (1oz) of the butter and a pinch of salt for 5 minutes, until transparent.
- Add the white wine and boil until reduced to nothing, now add the water and chicken stock and bring to the boil.
- Cook for about 10 minutes, then add the courgettes, French beans, peas and cabbage and cook for a further 5 minutes.
- Add the cream, whisk in the remaining butter and add the tomato and herbs.
- Season with salt, pepper and a pinch of sugar.
- Serve immediately.

Wine expert Susy Atkins's choice

Michael has given us a delightful, fresh, spring-like, herby soup and I'm going to choose an equally fresh, delicate white wine to go with it.

I'm going to go for a cooler climate area – Europe – and something more subtle and refined. This is a really classy wine which is a notch up from your everyday Italian wine. On the nose I get pears, apples and lemons – it is subtle but fruity too. That fresh fruit really comes through on the palate and goes well with the herby quality in the soup. At the end there is a soft roundness which complements the cream element in the soup.

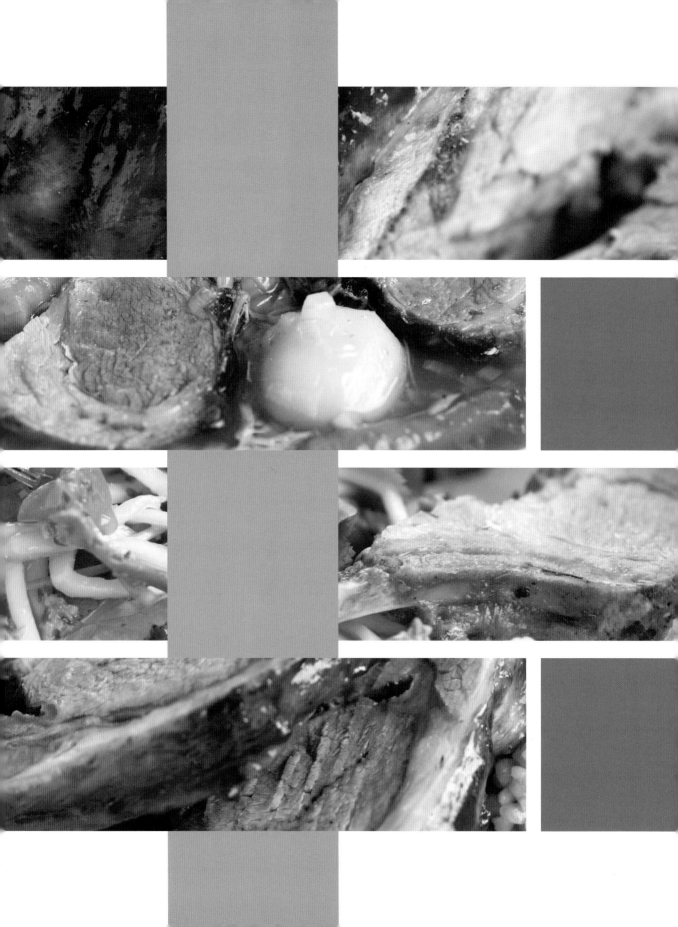

Best

Lamb & Mutton

roast rack of lamb in Irish stew consommé

Kevin Dundon

Serves 4

Ingredients

For the consommé

1 kg (2lb 2oz) scrag end of neck
  of lamb bones

1 leek, roughly chopped

2 carrots, roughly chopped

1 large onion, finely diced

2 celery sticks, roughly chopped

1 large bay leaf

1 large fresh thyme sprig

a small handful of flat-leaf
  parsley stalks

a few black peppercorns

For the stew

2 x seven-bone best end of lamb
  (each about 275–350g/10–12oz)

175g (6oz) small carrots

275g (10oz) baby new potatoes

1 tablespoon olive oil

1 leek, finely julienned

fresh rosemary sprigs, to garnish

Method

- Place the lamb bones in a large stockpot.
- Cover the leek, carrots, half of the onion, celery, herbs and peppercorns with at least 1¾ litres (3 pints) of cold water.
- Bring to the boil, season lightly and then simmer gently, uncovered, for about 2 hours until reduced by nearly two-thirds. You'll need 450ml (16fl oz) of stock in total. Skim off any grease that rises to the surface with a large spoon.
- Strain the stock through a fine sieve into a large jug and ideally leave to cool overnight so that you can scrape off any settled fat on top.
- To prepare the stew, preheat the oven to 200°C/400°F/Gas Mark 6.
- Season the racks of lamb and place in a small roasting tin.
- Roast for 20–25 minutes, or a little longer, depending on how pink you like your lamb.
- Remove from the oven and set aside to rest for 10–15 minutes.
- Peel and shape the carrots and baby potatoes into neat barrels, then add to the lamb stock with the remaining onion and bring to a simmer.
- Cook gently for 10–15 minutes until the potatoes are completely tender but are still holding their shape. Season to taste.
- Meanwhile, heat the oil in a frying pan. Add the julienned leek and sauté for 3 minutes until softened but not coloured. Season to taste.
- To serve, place the leek julienne in the centre of each serving bowl and spoon around the Irish stew consommé. Carve the rested racks of lamb into chops, arrange on top and garnish with rosemary sprigs.

Wine expert Susy Atkins's choice

Berberana Dragon Tempranillo

This wine has big strawberry aromas and oak that gives it a spicy layer. It certainly has the strength of character to go with the lamb dish.

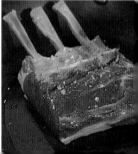

Patagonian lamb adobo
Si King

Serves 4

Ingredients

20g (¾oz) dried porcini mushrooms,
    soaked and chopped
2 teaspoons red wine vinegar
1 onion, very finely chopped
3 cloves garlic, crushed
1 teaspoon finely chopped
    fresh rosemary
1 tablespoon finely chopped
    flat-leaf parsley
½ teaspoon dried oregano
½ teaspoon sugar
½ teaspoon salt
½ teaspoon ground black pepper
250g (9oz) thin streaky bacon,
    or pancetta
2 lamb loin fillets, trimmed

To serve

mashed potatoes
roasted root vegetables, such
    as carrots or parsnips

Method

- Preheat the oven to 180°C/350°F/Gas Mark 4.
- Place the mushrooms, vinegar, onion, garlic, rosemary, parsley, oregano, sugar, salt and pepper in a blender and blitz to a paste.
- On a chopping board, spread a sheet of cling film, then place half the bacon rashers side by side on top to form a sheet.
- Place a lamb fillet over the ends of the rashers, so you're ready to roll it up.
- Spread half of the adobo paste evenly over the top of the fillet.
- Wrap the fillet up in the bacon sheet to form a roll using the cling film to help.
- Repeat the process with the second fillet.
- Discard the cling film.
- Place the two fillets in a roasting tin, making sure the rasher ends are tucked under the fillet on the bottom of the tin, and place in the oven for 15–25 minutes, depending on how you like your lamb.
- Remove from the oven and rest for 5–10 minutes.
- Serve sliced with the mashed potatoes and root vegetables.

Wine expert Jancis Robinson's choice
Tesco Finest Shiraz

This Patagonian lamb is quite difficult to match wine to because you've got the sweetness of the lamb and the salty crust of the bacon.

    This is a serious Argentinian wine – very spicy, lots of depth, really complex. It has the sweetness we are looking for, but it is not simple, light sweetness; it is concentrated, wild sweetness. It has that great velvety texture that all Argentinian reds have.

stir-fried sweet potatoes with lamb and green beans

Sophie Grigson

Serves 2–3

Ingredients

2 tablespoons sunflower
   or vegetable oil

1 x 2cm piece of fresh root ginger,
   peeled and chopped

2 cloves garlic, finely chopped

1 or 2 red chillies, deseeded and
   cut into strips

400g (14oz) sweet potato, peeled,
   thinly sliced and then quartered

125g (4½oz) green beans, topped
   and tailed and cut in half

225g (8oz) tender boneless lamb,
   cut into thin slivers

3 tablespoons black bean sauce

1 teaspoon toasted sesame oil

Method

- Place a large wok over a high heat.
- Once it starts to smoke, add the sunflower oil, then add the ginger, garlic and chillies and stir fry for 20 seconds or so.
- Next add the sweet potato and stir fry briskly for 3 minutes.
- Add the green beans and stir fry for 4–5 minutes, until the sweet potato is tender and the beans are patched with brown.
- Tip all the vegetables out on to a plate and return the wok to the heat.
- When it is back up to prime heat, add the lamb and stir fry for about 1 minute, until just barely cooked through.
- Return the vegetables to the wok and mix them well with the lamb.
- Add the black bean sauce and stir fry for a final couple of minutes.
- Stir in the sesame oil.
- Taste and add a little more black bean sauce if you think it needs it.

Wine expert Peter Richards's choice

Abadengo

Sophie's stir fry is an intriguing fusion: classic British cuisine with a modern Asian twist. That gives us an interesting range of flavours, from the meatiness and earthiness of the lamb and the sweet potatoes through to the savouriness of the black bean sauce.

This wine is full of individuality and character. The aromas are the classic Spanish ones of ripe fruit and sweet spice, but you also get a real savoury note in there too. On the palate it is dense and herbal and meaty, which is going to go really well with the unusual flavours in this dish.

grilled rack of lamb with mango salad and mint chutney

Atul Kochhar

Serves 4

Ingredients

For the lamb

1 tablespoon minced raw papaya

1 tablespoon minced garlic

1 teaspoon minced green chillies

1 teaspoon fennel seed powder

1 teaspoon black pepper powder

1 teaspoon sweet paprika

3 tablespoons mustard oil

100ml (3½fl oz) single cream

50ml (2fl oz) double cream

2 tablespoons gram flour

2 tablespoons Pernod or Ricard

½ nutmeg, grated

pinch of salt

2 x eight-bone lamb racks, excess
    fat removed

50g (2oz) butter, melted

For the mint chutney

200g (7oz) mint leaves

2 tablespoons chopped red onions

2 tablespoons lemon juice

1 green chilli

½ teaspoon salt

½ tablespoon vegetable oil

4 tablespoons thick Greek yoghurt

For the mango salad

2 green mangoes, julienned

several sprigs of coriander

1 bunch of watercress

1 teaspoon grated ginger

1 teaspoon toasted, crushed cumin

1 tablespoon lime juice

1 tablespoon olive oil

½ teaspoon sugar

Method

- Whisk all the ingredients for the lamb marinade together, rub onto the lamb and set aside to marinate for 2 hours.
- Preheat the oven to 200°C/400°F/Gas Mark 6.
- Remove the lamb from the marinade, shaking off the excess marinade, and place in a roasting tin.
- Cook for 12–15 minutes, then baste with the marinade and return to the oven to cook for a further 2–3 minutes.
- Remove the lamb from the oven and baste with the melted butter.
- Set aside and keep warm until ready to serve.
- Meanwhile, prepare the chutney. Bring a small pan of water to the boil, then drop in the mint leaves and return to the boil.
- Drain and refresh in iced water, then drain once more.
- Place the mint leaves in a food processor with the remaining chutney ingredients and blend to a fine purée.
- To make the salad, mix all the ingredients together and toss to combine.
- To serve, carve the lamb into portions and serve with a good spoonful of salad and a dollop of mint chutney.

Wine expert Peter Richards's choice

Casillero del Diablo Shiraz Rosé

With a delicious grilled rack of lamb, my first thought would be a red wine, but with a spicy dish like this, you should avoid tannin and oak and go for something fruity and fresh. Our best option by far would be a rosé.

This dish is complex, so you can't possibly hope to find a wine that will match up perfectly. You have to look at the bigger picture. What this wine does first and foremost is refresh the palate. It also has lovely touches of herbs and spices that are going to go really well with the mint and chilli.

masala mutton shanks with lemon rice

Ben O'Donoghue

Serves 4

Ingredients

For the curry

4 mutton shanks

1 tablespoon ground turmeric

1 x 3cm piece of root ginger, grated

3 cloves garlic, crushed

2 tablespoons sunflower oil

1 bay leaf

1 cinnamon stick

5 cloves

6 cardamom pods, bashed

2 onions, sliced

1 x 400g (14oz) tin chopped tomatoes

2 teaspoons ground cumin

3 teaspoons ground coriander

1 small bunch of coriander,
    roughly chopped

2 green chillies, halved

For the curry paste

50g (2oz) desiccated coconut

3 tablespoons coriander seeds

5 tablespoons poppy seeds

2 tablespoons fennel seeds

1 tablespoon black peppercorns

5 red chillies

For the rice

2 tablespoons sunflower oil

1 teaspoon mustard seeds

2 teaspoons chana dal

3 tablespoons cashew nuts

5g (¼oz) curry leaves

1 teaspoon turmeric

1 teaspoon asafoetida

1 teaspoon ground ginger

500g (1lb 2oz) cooked basmati rice

juice of 1 lemon

1 bunch of coriander

Method

· Place the mutton in a large pan with the turmeric, ginger, garlic and some salt. Add enough water to cover and simmer gently for 1½ hours, or until tender.

· Meanwhile, grind the curry paste ingredients together in a spice grinder or pestle and mortar.

· Heat the sunflower oil in a deep frying pan and add the bay leaf, cinnamon, cloves and cardamom and fry until aromatic.

· Add the onion and fry until it starts to soften.

· Add the tomato and cook for 5 minutes, then add the cumin, both lots of coriander and green chillies and cook for 3 minutes.

· Add the curry paste and cook for 2 minutes, then add the cooked mutton, some salt and enough of the cooking water to come halfway up the shanks.

· Cook for 20 minutes, turning the shanks over several times and adding more water if the sauce gets too thick.

· To make the rice, heat a frying pan until hot and add the sunflower oil.

· Add the mustard seeds and chana dal and fry until they start to pop.

· Add the cashew nuts, curry leaves, turmeric, asafoetida and ginger and stir fry for 1–2 minutes.

· Finally add the rice and lemon juice and heat through until hot.

· Serve the mutton with a spoonful of rice and sprinkle with coriander leaves.

Wine expert Peter Richards's choice

Sunrise Merlot

With curry, you don't want a red wine with lots of tannin and oak, as that is going to clash with those spicy curry flavours. I've found a complete bargain that I cannot ignore. The Sunrise Merlot from Chile is sleek and smooth, but also peppery and spicy.

lamb rack in a Japanese hot pepper paste with sesame spinach

Nic Watt

Serves 4

Ingredients

For the lamb

250g (9oz) hot-pepper paste
  (gochugang paste)

75ml (3fl oz) sake

25ml (1fl oz) soy sauce

75ml (3fl oz) mirin

1 pinch dried chilli

40g (1½oz) garlic paste

40g (1½oz) ginger paste

2 teaspoons toasted sesame oil

4 x four-bone lamb racks

1 tablespoon olive oil

For the sesame spinach

15g (½oz) toasted sesame seeds

60g (2oz) sesame paste

10g (½oz) sweet white miso

1 teaspoon ginger juice

45ml (1¾fl oz) dashi

2 teaspoons rice vinegar

a good squeeze of lemon juice

2 teaspoons sesame oil

500g (1lb 2oz) spinach leaves

1 pinch yama gobo (Japanese
  burdock root)

Method

- Place the hot pepper paste, sake, soy, mirin, dried chilli, garlic paste, ginger paste and toasted sesame oil in a bowl and whisk together to form a smooth paste.
- Wrap each protruding lamb bone in a piece of tin foil and pinch tight.
- Lightly brush the lamb racks with some of the hot-pepper marinade and place in the fridge, preferably for 24 hours. Retain the remaining marinade.
- Preheat the oven to 180°C/350°F/Gas Mark 4.
- Heat a frying pan until hot and add the olive oil and lamb.
- Seal on each side, then brush with more of the marinade.
- Place in the oven for 10–12 minutes. Remove and rest for 5 minutes.
- To prepare the spinach, place the sesame seeds, sesame paste, sweet white miso, ginger juice, dashi, rice vinegar, lemon juice and sesame oil in a bowl and whisk together.
- Heat a frying pan until hot, add the spinach and cook until wilted.
- Add the yama gobo and the dressing and mix to combine.
- To serve, spoon the spinach into the centre of a plate.
- Slice the lamb and serve with a little extra marinade on the plate.

Wine expert Olly Smith's choice

Ravenswood Lodi Zinfandel

This wine has got so much complexity. It has been snuggling down into those barrels, giving it an extra dimension that is savoury-tastic.

This wine has power, but it is not about brawn or brutality – it is about lasting flavour. This is Paula Radcliffe on rollerskates. You give her a push and she keeps on going, and that is brilliant for this dish as I want all those fantastic ingredients to shine through – miso, ginger, mirin, garlic and the texture of the sesame oil.

glazed pot roast shoulder of lamb with a crisp salad and buckwheat kasha

Martin Blunos

Serves 6–8

Ingredients

For the lamb

2 medium onions, peeled and cut
  into thick slices

1 large celery stalk, trimmed and
  cut into large chunks

1 large carrot, peeled, trimmed
  and cut into large chunks

1 large garlic head, cut in half

1 sprig of rosemary

1 x shoulder of lamb, boned, trimmed
  of excess fat, rolled and tied
    (1.5kg/3lb or more in weight)

6 x tinned anchovies in oil

250ml (9fl oz) white wine

300ml (11fl oz) chicken stock

150ml (5fl oz) double cream

juice of 1 lemon

For the glaze

1 tablespoon tomato ketchup

1 tablespoon tomato purée

1 tablespoon runny honey

1 tablespoon dark soy sauce

1 tablespoon malt vinegar

1 tablespoon Worcestershire sauce

1 tablespoon syrup from a jar of
  preserved ginger

For the kasha

250g (9oz) bulghar wheat

450ml (16fl oz) hot chicken stock

90g (3oz) unsalted butter

To serve

green salad

Method

- Preheat the oven to 150°C/300°F/Gas Mark 2.
- Place all the vegetables and the rosemary in a deep pan.
- Stab the tied joint in several places with the point of a sharp knife.
- Tear the anchovies in half and push into the openings on the joint.
- Put the joint on top of the vegetables in the pan, then pour over some of the anchovy oil and rub in well. Season with pepper.
- Pour the wine and stock around the joint, then cover the pan with foil or a tight-fitting lid. Place on the heat and bring to the boil, then transfer to the oven and cook for about 1½ hrs, or until the meat is tender.
- Remove from the oven. Remove the joint and place on a roasting tin.
- Turn the oven up to 230°C/450°F/Gas Mark 8.
- Place all the glaze ingredients into a bowl and mix well.
- Brush the glaze over the joint, then place in the oven for 12–15 minutes. Reduce the heat if the meat is colouring too quickly.
- Remove from the oven and set aside, keeping warm.
- Pass the initial cooking juices through a sieve into a small saucepan, skim off the fat and boil rapidly to reduce a little. When reduced, add the cream and lemon juice and check the seasoning.
- Meanwhile, prepare the kasha. Preheat the oven to 200°C/400°F/Gas Mark 6.
- Heat a frying pan until hot, then add the bulghar wheat and toast for a few minutes. Add the stock, season with salt and black pepper and dot with a third of the butter.
- Cover with a lid, place in the oven and cook for about 20 minutes, until the stock is completely absorbed.
- Remove from the oven and fork through the remaining butter.
- To serve, remove the string from the joint and cut into thick slices. Spoon some bulghar wheat onto each plate and top with slices of lamb. Spoon the sauce over the top and serve with a green salad.

roasted chump of lamb with rustic ratatouille

Galton Blackiston

Serves 4

Ingredients

For the lamb

2 well-trimmed chumps of lamb,
   all fat removed
25ml (1fl oz) olive oil
25g (1oz) butter

For the rustic ratatouille

1 red onion, cut into wedges
1 large aubergine, cut into chunks
1 yellow pepper, cut into chunks
1 red pepper, cut into chunks
2 courgettes, cut into chunks
1 small fennel bulb, cut into chunks
1 clove garlic, roughly chopped
150ml (5fl oz) olive oil
225g (8oz) baby vine tomatoes
15g (½oz) basil, roughly chopped
salt
black pepper

Method

- Preheat the oven to 220°C/425°F/Gas Mark 7.
- Heat a frying pan until hot, then add the olive oil and butter and allow to foam.
- Add the lamb, meat side down, and seal all over.
- Place the lamb on a trivet in a roasting tin, season well and roast for about 15–20 minutes for pink lamb, or for up to 30 minutes if you prefer your lamb more well done.
- Remove from the oven and keep warm for 5 minutes to allow the meat to rest before serving.
- To prepare the ratatouille, place all the ingredients except the tomatoes and basil, in a bowl and toss together with the olive oil.
- Season with salt and black pepper and place on a roasting tin.
- Place in the oven for 10 minutes, until just coloured.
- Add the tomatoes and basil and return to the oven for a further 20 minutes, until just tender but with a little bite.
- Check the seasoning.
- To serve, spoon the ratatouille into the centre of the plate (you can serve it either hot or cold). Cut the lamb into thick slices and lay across the ratatouille.

Wine expert Tim Atkin's choice

Denbies Redlands

This is just about as good as an English red wine gets. It's a pale, light-bodied to medium-bodied red with a soft style, and is lovely on the nose with its raspberry and wild strawberry notes. On the palate it is unoaked, not too alcoholic and the tannins are just right.

There is enough acidity in this wine to cope with the fat of the lamb, but at the same time it is soft enough to balance the acidity you're going to get in the ratatouille.

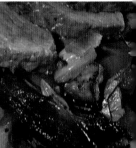

traditional Lancashire hotpot
James Martin

Serves 4

Ingredients

900g (2lb) best end and middle
  neck of British lamb, chopped into
  2½cm pieces
1 tablespoon groundnut oil
2 tablespoons butter
4 lamb kidneys, cored, skinned
  and chopped quite small
350g (12oz) onions, peeled and
  cut into 1cm wedges
1 clove garlic, roughly chopped
1 tablespoon flour
570ml (1 pint) fresh, hot beef stock
2 teaspoons Worcestershire sauce
1 bay leaf
2 sprigs of fresh thyme
900g (2lb) potatoes, peeled and
  cut into 5mm thick slices
salt
black pepper

Method

· Preheat the oven to 170°C/325°F/Gas Mark 3.
· Trim the lamb of any excess fat and pat dry with kitchen paper.
· Heat the oil in a large frying pan with half the butter until it is very hot,
  then brown the pieces of lamb, two or three at a time. As they cook,
  put them in a wide casserole dish (3½ litres/7 pints capacity).
· Brown the pieces of kidney too, and tuck these in among the meat.
· Fry the onions for 10 minutes until they turn brown at the edges.
· Stir in the flour to soak up the juices and gradually add the hot stock
  and Worcestershire sauce, stirring or whisking until the flour and
  liquid are smoothly blended. Season with salt and pepper, bring it up
  to simmering point, then pour it over the meat in the casserole dish.
· Add the bay leaf and thyme, then arrange the potato slices on top in
  an overlapping pattern.
· Season the potatoes and add a few dots of butter over the surface.
  Cover with a tight-fitting lid and cook for 1½ hours. You can brush the
  potatoes with a little more butter, then place under the grill to crisp up
  if you like.
· Remove the bay leaf and sprigs of thyme before serving.

Best

Beef & Venison

steak maman blanc with sauté potatoes
Raymond Blanc

Serves 2

Ingredients

For the steak

2 x 225g (8oz) sirloin steaks,
   2cm thick (preferably organic)
1 pinch of sea salt
1 teaspoon freshly ground
   black pepper
1 teaspoon olive oil
20g (¾oz) unsalted butter
110ml (4fl oz) water

For the potatoes

1 tablespoon olive oil
2 medium King Edward potatoes,
   cut into 2cm dice
2 pinches of sea salt
1 pinch of freshly ground black pepper
10g (½oz) unsalted butter
1 handful of flat-leaf parsley,
   roughly chopped
½ banana shallot, finely chopped

Method

- Season the steaks with the salt and pepper, pressing it firmly into the steaks on each side.
- Heat a large frying pan, add the oil and butter and heat until the butter is foaming, light-brown and smells nutty.
- Lay the steaks in the foaming butter and cook for 1½–2 minutes on each side for rare, 3 minutes for medium rare, or 4 minutes for medium.
- Transfer the steaks to a warm plate with tongs.
- Pour the water into the frying pan and scrape the base of the pan with a wooden spoon to release the caramelized residue, which will give taste and colour to this succulent juice, and simmer for 1 minute to emulsify.
- To prepare the potatoes, heat a frying pan until hot and add the olive oil and potatoes.
- Fry over a medium heat until golden-brown and tender – about 4–5 minutes.
- Season with the salt and pepper, then reduce the heat and add the butter, parsley and shallot. Cook until the butter has melted and glazed the potatoes and the shallot has warmed through.
- To serve, place the steaks onto plates, pour the juice over the top and serve with the potatoes alongside.

Wine expert Tim Atkin's choice

Argento Malbec

What we need with this dish is a fairly robust, even tannic wine. Argento Malbec is perfect – rich, fruity and with robust tannins. It is produced against the flank of the Andes, in a warm area of Argentina, and has flavours of ripe blackcurrant, plums, a little bit of licorice and just an undertone of oak. It is a fantastic wine which just cries out for a piece of steak.

collops of beef with whisky and mushroom cream, wilted spinach and crushed tatties

Nick Nairn

Serves 4

Ingredients

For the beef

3 tablespoons black peppercorns

4 x 175g (6oz) fillet steaks

4 teaspoons Dijon mustard

sea salt and black pepper,
    freshly ground

2 tablespoons sunflower oil

50g (2oz) butter

200g (7oz) fresh cep mushrooms
    when available, or wild mushrooms,
        thickly sliced

50ml (2fl oz) whisky

50ml (2fl oz) beef stock

50ml (2fl oz) double cream

For the tatties

450g (1lb) new potatoes, scrubbed

50g (2oz) butter

3 tablespoons chopped flat-leaf parsley

salt and white pepper, freshly ground

For the spinach

25g (1oz) butter

500g (1lb 2oz) baby leaf spinach

3 tablespoons water

sea salt and white pepper,
    freshly ground

Method

· Put a pan of water on a high heat. When boiling, add the potatoes and turn down to a simmer.

· Use a pepper grinder on a coarse setting to grind the peppercorns, and spread over a small plate.

· Cut the steaks in half along the equator to make four thin medallions.

· Smear all sides of the steaks with the Dijon mustard, then press them into the crushed peppercorns to coat.

· You can now season the steak with salt, if needed – adding salt before this stage draws out the moisture from the meat, preventing the pepper from sticking.

· Heat a large frying pan until hot and add the sunflower oil and then the steaks. Turn once to brown both sides. Don't fiddle with them once they are in the pan or the peppercorn crust will fall off – the aim is to produce a good crusty coating on each surface.

· Now add the butter and allow it to colour a nut brown, but don't let it burn.

· Add the mushrooms and work around in the butter. As the mushrooms start to absorb the juices, turn the steaks again and allow them to cook for three or four minutes on both sides, moving them around the pan to make sure the whole surface has plenty of colour and the edges of the meat are well sealed.

· Transfer the steaks to a baking tray and leave in a warm place.

· When the potatoes are tender, drain and place in a large mixing bowl.

· Add the butter and gently crush each potato with the back of a fork until it just splits. Add the parsley and season.

· Mix until all the butter has been absorbed, but don't overwork.

collops of beef with whisky and mushroom cream, wilted spinach and crushed tatties (cont)

Method (cont)

- Meanwhile, prepare the spinach. Heat a medium frying pan or wok until hot.
- Add the butter and toss in the spinach. Mix well and then add the water. Continue to stir until wilted.
- Remove from the heat, season and set aside until ready to serve.
- Add the whisky to the pan used to cook the steaks, and cook over a very high heat for 1 minute to boil off the alcohol. A word of warning – the whisky is likely to burst into flames. If this worries you, have a large lid handy to whack on the pan.
- Add the stock and reduce until really thick, then pour in the cream.
- Reduce again, scraping and stirring together any gooey bits from the bottom of the pan.
- When it boils fiercely, it's ready. Pour any juices from the resting meat into the sauce.
- To serve, use a chef's ring to make a little pile of potatoes in the middle of each plate.
- Sit a little pile of spinach on the potatoes and two medallions of steak on top of that.
- Spoon the mushroom sauce over the steak.

Wine expert Olly Smith's choice

Tinto da Anfora, Alentejano

I'm hunting for a red wine with enough spice to match up to the peppercorns and enough body to cope with the might of the cow. Tinto da Anfora has brutish elegance and charm – it's James Bond in a bottle.

This wine is so big, but it needs to be because there are so many big flavours in this dish – mustard, spice, whisky and the oomph of the udder. It's got high alcohol – 14 per cent – but it's also got wonderful rich fruit, fantastic acidity and great tannins.

beef sausage toad-in-the-hole with my mum's onion gravy

James Martin

Serves 4–6

Ingredients

For the toad

225g (8oz) plain flour
8 eggs
570ml (1 pint) milk
1 tablespoon olive oil
6 beef sausages
75g (3oz) beef dripping
2 sprigs of thyme, leaves picked

For the gravy

50g (2oz) butter
2 onions, sliced
1 tablespoon beef Bisto powder
1 tablespoon Marmite
400ml (14fl oz) vegetable stock
salt
black pepper

Method

- Place the flour in a bowl and make a well in the centre.
- Whisk in the eggs and milk and continue to whisk to a smooth batter.
- Place in the fridge overnight.
- Preheat the oven to 220°C/425°F/Gas Mark 7.
- Heat a frying pan until hot, then add the olive oil and sausages and seal on each side until brown. Put the beef dripping in a roasting tin and place in the oven until the fat has totally melted and the tray is hot.
- Remove the batter from the fridge and whisk once more to combine.
- Add the thyme leaves and season.
- Place the sausages in the roasting tin and pour over the batter.
- Place in the oven for 35–40 minutes.
- Open the oven door to let out the steam, then lower the temperature to 180°C/350°F/Gas Mark 4 and cook for a further 10 minutes.
- Remove from the oven and stand for a few minutes.
- To make the gravy, heat a frying pan until hot, add most of the butter and all the onions and cook for 10 minutes until nicely soft.
- Add the Bisto and Marmite. Stir to combine. Add the stock, bring to the boil, then reduce the heat and simmer for 5 minutes until thickened.
- Season with salt and black pepper and finish with a knob of butter.

braciole in tomato sauce with green salad and oranges with cracked pepper

Adriana Trigiani

Serves 6–8

Ingredients

For the tomato sauce

1kg (2lb 2oz) tomatoes, puréed

175g (6oz) tomato paste

425ml (15fl oz) water

1 teaspoon garlic salt

1 teaspoon freshly ground black
  pepper

1 tablespoon olive oil

1 tablespoon mixed herbs

110–175g (4–6oz) pork bone with
  a little meat left on

¼ teaspoon salt

For the braciole

900g (2lb) top round steak, 5mm
  thick, cut into 4 x 15cm slices

1 large bunch of flat-leaf parsley,
  roughly chopped

1 small bunch of basil leaves, roughly
  chopped

150g (5oz) dried breadcrumbs

3 tablespoons finely chopped garlic

150g (5oz) Parmesan cheese,
  freshly grated

75ml (3fl oz) olive oil

1 tablespoon balsamic vinegar

a large handful of mixed green leaves

For the salad

3 large oranges

3 tablespoons olive oil

freshly ground black pepper

2 tablespoons extra virgin olive oil

Method

· Place the tomato purée, tomato paste and water in a large saucepan and bring to a simmer. Add the garlic salt, pepper and half the olive oil and stir well. Add the mixed herbs and stir well once more.

· Heat a frying pan until hot, then add the remaining olive oil and sauté the pork bone with the salt until browned.

· Add the pork bone to the sauce. Return to a simmer and cook for 3–4 hours over a low heat. Once ready, remove the pork bone from the sauce and discard.

· While the sauce is cooking, prepare the braciole. Pound the meat to tenderize it and make it thin (avoid making any holes). Blend the parsley and the basil and spread the mixture on the meat. Mix the breadcrumbs with the garlic and sprinkle that over the herb mixture on the meat.

· Add the cheese on top of the breadcrumb mixture and season.

· Roll the meat up into pinwheels, tucking in the ends and securing with twine.

· Heat a frying pan until medium hot and add the olive oil and meat and seal on each side until just coloured.

· Transfer the meat to the pan of tomato sauce and simmer slowly for 45–60 minutes, until the meat is tender.

· Remove the meat from the pan and place on a cutting board.

· Remove the twine and let the meat cool for about 5 minutes, then cut into 5cm thick slices.

· To prepare the salad, peel the oranges and cut them into 5mm thick slices, removing the pips.

· Place the oranges on a plate and drizzle with olive oil and black pepper.

· Whisk the extra virgin olive oil and balsamic vinegar together and toss with the salad leaves.

· To serve, place several slices of meat onto a plate with a drizzle of tomato sauce, some orange slices and some dressed salad leaves.

meatballs with eggs on top
Si King

Serves 4

Ingredients

For the meatballs

500g (1lb 2oz) minced beef

1 onion, very finely chopped

3 cloves garlic, crushed

1 teaspoon ground ginger

1 teaspoon ground cumin

½ teaspoon chilli powder

1 teaspoon paprika

a small handful of finely chopped
    coriander leaves

a small handful of finely chopped
    flat-leaf parsley

1 egg yolk

salt

black pepper

For the sauce

2 tablespoons olive oil

1 small onion, finely chopped

2 tablespoons tomato purée

1 x 400g (14oz) tin of chopped
    tomatoes, drained of excess juice

2 teaspoons honey

200g (7oz) frozen peas

4 free-range eggs

chopped parsley, to garnish

Method

- First, construct your meatballs. In a big bowl, mix together the beef, onion, garlic, spices, fresh herbs, egg yolk and some salt and pepper. Get your hands in it to knead it all together and form a smooth paste, then shape into walnut-sized balls and set aside.
- To prepare the sauce, heat up the olive oil in a tagine or casserole dish and cook the onion slowly over a low heat until translucent.
- Add the meatballs and brown lightly over a medium-high heat.
- Stir the tomato purée into the tomatoes and add to the tagine along with the honey.
- Cover and simmer for 10 minutes.
- Stir in the peas, then break the eggs on top of the stew, turn the heat right down and cook with the lid on until you have the eggs how you like them.
- Garnish with a little parsley and serve.

Wine expert Olly Smith's choice

Castillo La Paz Tempranillo

I am looking for a red wine with a decent wollop of fruit, but I don't want to over-rev the texture. I want to work with the squidgy, voluptuous nature of this dish.

   If you like rioja, you will love this wine, as it is made from the same grape variety. There is a lot of heat and ripeness in the glass. You immediately get hot fruit, raisins and prunes leaping out at you. The sweetness of the fruit is going to pick up on the honey, the tomatoes and the meat. This wine is not going to swamp the dish and will work beautifully with the eggs. It has both body and elegance, like Rambo ice-dancing with Torvill and Dean.

pan-fried calves' liver with Swiss chard
Theo Randall

Serves 4

Ingredients

110g (4oz) puy lentils
2 cloves garlic
4 sage leaves
juice of ½ lemon
4 tablespoons extra virgin olive oil
4 large chard leaves, sliced 1cm thick
½ teaspoon dried chilli flakes
50g (2oz) unsalted butter
8 slices smoked pancetta
8 sage leaves
4 x 1cm thick slices calves' liver
4 tablespoons balsamic vinegar
4 tablespoons crème fraîche

Method

· Place the lentils, 1 garlic clove and four sage leaves in a saucepan and cover with water.
· Bring to a boil. Reduce the heat and simmer for 30 minutes until tender.
· Drain and return to the saucepan.
· Season and add the lemon juice and half the olive oil, then keep warm.
· Bring a saucepan of salted water to the boil, add the leaves and stalk from the chard and cook for 1–2 minutes until tender.
· Drain and set aside.
· Heat a frying pan until hot and add the remaining olive oil and garlic and the chilli flakes, along with the chard.
· Stir fry for 1 minute, then set aside and keep warm.
· Heat a large frying pan, add the butter, pancetta and 8 sage leaves, and cook for 2 minutes until crispy.
· Add the liver and cook for a further 1 minute on each side.
· Remove from the pan and set aside.
· Pour any excess fat out of the pan, add the balsamic vinegar and crème fraîche and cook for 1 minute, whisking to combine.
· To serve, place some calves' liver and braised chard on each plate, top with a spoonful of lentils and spoon over the balsamic sauce.

Wine expert Tim Atkin's choice

Langhe Nebbiolo De Forville

What we need here is a red wine with what Australians call 'a little bit of a grunt' – that's to say, with some good fruitiness but also some tannin.

My choice has got to be an Italian red. This wine is pale in colour, but really packs a tannic punch. It's got lovely perfumes on the nose – roses and a little bit of red cherry. On the palate, it has quite good acidity, but it is the tannin which really kicks in with this wine and that is why you always have to serve it with food.

venison with juniper berries, sour cherry sauce and pumpkin mash

Silvena Rowe

Serves 6

Ingredients

For the venison

6 x 150g (5oz) venison medallions

200ml (7fl oz) red wine

4–6 sprigs of fresh thyme

4–6 sprigs of fresh rosemary

1 clove garlic, peeled and crushed

1 small shallot, peeled and
finely chopped

1 small carrot, peeled and
finely chopped

1 celery stalk, finely chopped

8 white peppercorns

10 juniper berries, crushed

2 tablespoons grape seed oil

For the sauce

20g (¾oz) butter

300g (11oz) fresh or frozen cherries,
stones removed

2 teaspoons redcurrant jelly

½ teaspoon chopped fresh thyme

110ml (4fl oz) good chicken stock

For the mash

600g (1lb 5oz) King Edward potatoes,
peeled and chopped

600g (1lb 5oz) pumpkin or butternut
squash, peeled and chopped

5 tablespoons extra virgin olive oil

Method

- Place all the marinade ingredients except the grape seed oil in a large container, mix well and place the venison medallions in this to marinate overnight.
- Preheat the oven to 200°C/400°F/Gas Mark 6.
- Remove the venison from the marinade (reserving this) and dry well.
- Lightly brush the meat with some grape seed oil and season.
- Heat a frying pan until hot, then add the remaining grape seed oil and the venison.
- Seal on each side, then place in the oven for 10–12 minutes for just pink, or longer if you like it medium to well done.
- Meanwhile, prepare the sauce. Using the pan that the venison was cooked in, melt the butter and sauté the vegetables from the marinade, reserving the liquid marinade.
- Add the cherries, redcurrant jelly, thyme, stock and half of the marinade liquor. Reduce by half, then pass through a fine sieve.
- Add the cherries back in and season.
- To prepare the mash, place the potato and pumpkin in a large saucepan and cover with salted water.
- Bring to the boil and simmer for 15 minutes until tender.
- Drain, return to the saucepan and place back on the heat to drive off the extra moisture. Add the olive oil, mash until smooth and season.
- To serve, slice the medallions horizontally and place on top of the mash on each plate. Spoon the sour cherry sauce over the venison.

Wine expert Susy Atkins's choice
Heartland Dolcetto Lagrein

On the palate this wine is dense and herbal and meaty, which is going to go really well with the unusual flavours in this dish.

braised beef short ribs with Innis and Gunn beer, salsify and bashed neeps

Mark Hix

Serves 4

Ingredients

For the ribs

2kg (4lb 4oz) beef short ribs, cut
   through the bone to about 10cm
   lengths

2 tablespoons flour

2 onions, roughly chopped

2 celery sticks, roughly chopped

1 carrot, peeled and roughly chopped

1 teaspoon tomato purée

330ml (11½fl oz) Innis and Gunn beer

2 litres (3½ pints) beef stock

3 cloves garlic, chopped

1 bay leaf

a few sprigs of thyme

5 black peppercorns

For the salsify

6–8 sticks of salsify, peeled and cut
   at an angle into 2–3cm pieces

25g (1oz) butter

1 tablespoon chopped parsley

For the bashed neeps

400g (14oz) turnips, peeled and
   cut into chunks

50g (2oz) butter

Method

- Preheat the oven to 220°C/425°F/Gas Mark 7.
- Season the ribs and dust them with 1 tablespoon of the flour.
- Place them in a roasting tin in the oven with the onion, celery and carrot for 30–40 minutes, turning every so often, until nicely browned.
- Transfer the vegetables and ribs to a heavy-bottomed saucepan, leaving any fat in the pan. Add the rest of the flour and the tomato purée to the roasting tin and stir over a low heat for 1 minute.
- Gradually add the beer and beef stock, stirring well to avoid lumps.
- Bring to the boil, then add to the saucepan. Add the garlic, bay leaf, thyme and peppercorns, season, cover and simmer gently for 1¾–2 hours, or until the meat is tender.
- Remove the ribs and vegetables from the sauce, discarding the vegetables and setting the ribs aside. Continue to simmer the sauce until it thickens to a rich, gravy-like consistency.
- Meanwhile, place the salsify in a saucepan of salted water and bring to the boil. Reduce the heat and simmer for 6–8 minutes until tender.
- Drain and toss in the butter and parsley and season to taste.
- For the turnips, place them in a saucepan of water and bring to the boil, then reduce the heat and simmer for 10–15 minutes until tender.
- Drain and return to the pan along with the butter. Using a masher, mash the turnips to a purée, then season to taste.
- To serve, reheat the ribs in the sauce, then serve with a spoonful of bashed neeps, the salsify and a generous spoonful of sauce.

Wine expert Susie Barrie's choice

Les Perdrigolles Crozes-Hermitage

This wine has meaty, rustic, red-berry flavours that are perfect with the slow-cooked beef and beer. It is a wintry wine to go with a fantastic wintry dish.

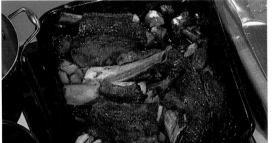

beef, asparagus and mangetout stir fry

Daniel Galmiche

Serves 2

Ingredients

150g (5oz) Scotch beef fillet, thinly sliced

20ml (¾fl oz) sake

20ml (¾fl oz) soy sauce

1 teaspoon grated fresh ginger

½ teaspoon soft brown sugar

½ clove garlic, finely chopped

1 small red chilli

110g (4oz) asparagus, julienned

75g (3oz) mangetout, julienned

2 teaspoons sesame oil

2 teaspoons sesame seeds

1 sprig of fresh coriander

Method

- Place the beef, sake, soy sauce, ginger, sugar, garlic and chilli in a bowl and mix to combine.
- Set aside to marinate for 30 minutes if you have the time.
- Heat a wok until hot and add the beef.
- Stir fry for 2 minutes until browned, then add the asparagus and mangetout.
- Continue to stir fry for a further 2–3 minutes, until the vegetables are just tender and the beef is cooked through.
- Add the sesame oil, then season with salt and black pepper.
- Place on a plate and garnish with the sesame seeds and coriander.

Wine expert Olly Smith's choice

Notios

I am looking for a red wine with low tannin and, crucially, some elegance because I don't want to swamp those fresh asparagus flavours and the mangetout. This one is perfect!

A lot of people wouldn't think of trying a Greek wine, but you should. You immediately get a fresh, fruity blueberry smell coming out of the glass. It's got just enough cherry zip to cut through the sesame oil.

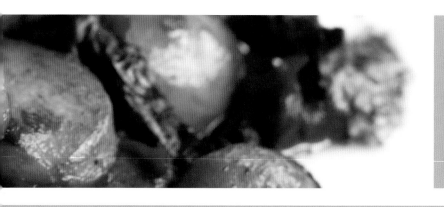

Best

Ham & Pork

hoisin and plum glazed ham with lemon potato salad

Bill Granger

Serves 6–8

Ingredients

For the ham

2–3kg (4lb 4oz–6lb 6oz) easy-carve cooked ham leg

75g (3oz) star anise, to decorate

125ml (4½fl oz) hoisin sauce

125ml (4½fl oz) plum sauce

60ml (2½fl oz) Chinese rice wine

60ml (2½fl oz) soy sauce

60g (2½oz) soft brown sugar

1 teaspoon Chinese five spice

For the potato salad

750g (1lb 11oz) waxy potatoes (such as kipfler), peeled and sliced

1 teaspoon sea salt

75ml (3fl oz) extra virgin olive oil

125ml (4½fl oz) lemon juice

1 tablespoon sumac (available in Middle Eastern grocers)

juice of 1 lime

1 small green pepper, finely diced

2 large red chillies, seeded and finely diced

1 small bunch of mint, roughly chopped

1 large bunch of flat-leaf parsley leaves

6 spring onions, finely sliced

Method

- Preheat the oven to 180°C/350°F/Gas Mark 4.
- Using a small, sharp knife cut through the rind around the shank of the ham. Carefully lift the rind from the fat in one piece and keep for storing.
- Score the white fat in a diamond pattern and press a star anise into the centre of every 2–3 diamonds.
- Place the ham on a rack over a roasting tin. Pour a small amount of water in the base of the tray to prevent the glaze from catching.
- Place the remaining ingredients in a saucepan over a low heat, stirring to combine and dissolve the sugar.
- Remove from the heat and pour the glaze over the ham, making sure that all the exposed fat is covered.
- Bake the ham for 30–40 minutes, basting until golden.
- Meanwhile, bring a large saucepan of water to the boil, then add the potatoes and salt, reduce the heat to medium and simmer for about 8–10 minutes until the potatoes are just undercooked (they will continue cooking when removed from the water).
- Place the olive oil, lemon and lime juice and sumac in a bowl, season and stir to combine. Pour half the dressing over the hot potatoes and stir.
- Leave to cool, then add the green pepper, chilli, mint, parsley, spring onion and the remaining dressing and stir gently.
- Serve hot or cold. To store the ham after carving, cover with the reserved rind, then wrap in a tea towel. Do not use cling film to cover the ham.

Wine expert Susie Barrie's choice

Peter Lehmann Riesling

This wine is refreshing and full of lime and crisp green apple flavours, which are going to work well with the hot and sour flavours in the potato salad.

pan-fried pork belly with scallops and squid, caramelized onions and balsamic sauce

Tom Aikens

Serves 4

Ingredients

For the pork belly

450g (1lb) pork belly

2 carrots, roughly chopped

1 onion, cut into quarters

4 cloves garlic

1 celery stick

1 small bunch of thyme

1 teaspoon coarse sea salt

½ teaspoon black peppercorns

1 tablespoon vegetable oil

For the caramelized onions

40g (1½oz) butter

2 onions, finely sliced

2 teaspoons caster sugar

2 sprigs of thyme

5 tablespoons balsamic vinegar

For the scallops and squid

25g (1oz) butter

4 banana shallots, finely diced

200ml (7fl oz) balsamic vinegar

250ml (9fl oz) fresh chicken stock

1 tablespoon vegetable oil

8 scallops, sliced in half

4 baby squid, finely sliced into rings

Method

- Place the pork belly in a large saucepan and cover with water.
- Bring to the boil, then drain, discarding the water, and return the pork belly to the pan. Cover with water once more, then add the carrot, onion, garlic, celery, thyme, salt and peppercorns.
- Bring to a boil, then reduce the heat and simmer for 2 hours.
- Remove from the pan and place on a plate. Place a tray on top and then a couple of tins on top of the tray. Place in the fridge for 1 hour until cold and pressed flat.
- Remove from the fridge and cut into 1.5cm thick slices.
- Heat a frying pan until hot, then add the vegetable oil.
- Season the pork slices and fry in the oil until crispy and golden.
- Meanwhile, heat a frying pan until hot and add the butter, onions, sugar and thyme. Cook over a gentle heat for 5–10 minutes until tender. Turn the heat up and colour the onions until just browned. Add the vinegar and reduce until it just coats the onions, then season.
- Heat a frying pan until hot and add the butter and shallots.
- Cook for 3–4 minutes. Add the vinegar and reduce by two-thirds.
- Add the stock, reduce again by two-thirds until sticky and season.
- Heat a frying pan until hot. Add the vegetable oil. Season the scallops and squid and add to the pan.
- Cook for 2 minutes, turning the scallops halfway through.
- To serve, place some of the pork belly on each plate. Top with the onions, 3 scallop pieces, then finish with the squid and sauce.

Wine expert Olly Smith's choice

Simonsig Chenin Blanc

This wine is so rich, which is going to work with the spring of the squid, the squidge of the scallop and the pudge of the pork. Terrific!

home-made pork sausages with colcannon and apple sauce

Rachel Allen

Serves 4

Ingredients

For the sausages

450g (1lb) fatty minced pork

50g (2oz) breadcrumbs

1 egg, whisked

1 clove garlic, peeled and crushed

1 tablespoon chopped fresh parsley
or marjoram

2 tablespoons olive or sunflower oil

salt

black pepper

For the colcannon

1½kg (3lb) floury potatoes, scrubbed

100g (3½oz) butter

500g (1lb 2oz) green cabbage,
outer leaves removed and
discarded, inner leaves sliced

250ml (9fl oz) hot milk

2 tablespoons chopped parsley

For the apple sauce

1 large cooking apple (350g/12oz),
peeled, cored and roughly chopped

1 tablespoon water

25–50g (1–2oz) caster sugar

Method

- Place all the ingredients for the sausages except the olive oil in a bowl and mix thoroughly, then season with salt and pepper.
- Fry a tiny bit of the mixture in a pan with a little olive or sunflower oil and taste to check the seasoning.
- Divide the mixture into 12 pieces and shape each one into a sausage.
- Place on a baking tin or plate and set aside until you want to cook them. (Chill for a day in the fridge or freeze.)
- To cook the sausages, heat a frying pan on a low to medium heat, add the olive or sunflower oil and gently fry the sausages for 12–15 minutes until golden on all sides and cooked on the inside.
- To prepare the colcannon, cook the potatoes in boiling salted water until tender, draining three-quarters of the water after 5–10 minutes and continuing to cook over a low heat.
- When cooked, drain all the remaining water, then peel the potatoes and mash with half the butter while hot. I usually hold the potato on a fork and peel them with a knife if they are very hot.
- Heat a saucepan until hot and add the remaining butter, 2 tablespoons of water and the sliced cabbage.
- Toss over a medium heat for 5–7 minutes, until just cooked.
- Add to the potatoes, then add the hot milk and the parsley.
- Season and beat until smooth – add more milk if necessary.
- To make the apple sauce, place the apple in a small saucepan with the water, then put the lid on and cook over a gentle heat, stirring, until the apple has broken down to a mush. Add sugar to taste.
- To serve, add 3 sausages to each plate. Add a spoonful of colcannon with a knob of butter in the centre to melt, and some warm apple sauce.

rösti with black pudding and roasted apples
James Martin

Serves 2

Ingredients

600g (1lb 5oz) potatoes, peeled
   and grated
75g (3oz) crème fraîche
1 egg yolk
75g (3oz) melted butter
1 tablespoon olive oil
1 small black pudding, sliced
25g (1oz) butter
2 small Cox's apples, peeled,
   cored and cut into wedges
50ml (2fl oz) cider

Method

- Preheat the oven to 200°C/400°F/Gas Mark 6.
- Place the grated potatoes in a tea towel and squeeze out any excess water.
- Place in a bowl with the crème fraîche and egg yolk and season well, then stir to combine.
- Heat a frying pan until medium hot, then add the butter.
- Place 2 x 7cm metal rings in the pan.
- Spoon the potato mix into the rings and press down well with a spoon.
- Cook for 3–4 minutes until golden-brown, continuing to press down.
- Turn over and cook until golden-brown on the other side.
- Place in the oven for 5–10 minutes until tender and cooked through.
- Meanwhile, heat a small frying pan until hot, then add the black pudding and cook until browned and cooked through.
- Heat a further pan until hot and add the butter.
- Add the apple segments, toss in the butter and cook until golden.
- Add the cider and cook until totally reduced.
- Serve the rösti topped with the black pudding and the apples.

roast pork cutlet and crispy black pudding with a ragout of white bean and apple

Bryn Williams

Serves 4

Ingredients

2 tablespoons olive oil

4 x 160g (5½oz) pork cutlets

125g (4½oz) black pudding, cut into
    4 pieces, skin removed

110g (4oz) plain flour

2 eggs, beaten

110g (4oz) breadcrumbs

3 tablespoons butter

4 apples, peeled and cut into
    1cm cubes

1 x 400g (14oz) tin of white beans,
    drained and rinsed

400ml (14fl oz) chicken stock

75g (3oz) flat-leaf parsley, chopped

75ml (3fl oz) cider vinegar

Method

· Preheat the oven to 170°C/325°F/Gas Mark 3.

· Heat a frying pan until hot and add the olive oil.

· Season the pork cutlets, then place in the frying pan.

· Colour on both sides, then place in the oven for 6–8 minutes.

· Preheat a deep-fat fryer to 160°C/325°F.

· Mould the black pudding meat into 4 balls (they should be about the size of golf balls).

· Roll the balls in the flour, then in the beaten egg, then in the breadcrumbs so that they are completely coated.

· Deep fry for 3–4 minutes, or until golden-brown, then drain on kitchen paper.

· To make the ragout, melt 1 tablespoon of the butter in a pan over a very low heat, then add the diced apple and gently cook for 2–3 minutes, making sure the fruit does not colour.

· Add the white beans and the chicken stock and bring to the boil. Cook until the liquid has reduced by half, then add the remaining butter.

· Add the chopped parsley and cider vinegar and season to taste.

· To serve, pour some ragout into the bottom of 4 large bowls. Place a pork cutlet on top of each and a black pudding ball alongside.

Wine expert Olly Smith's choice

Secano Estate Pinot Noir Rosé

This wine has the right tang to pick up on the cider vinegar and the apple and has low tannin so it will match up with the pork. With just the right fruit, it balances up with the black pudding and cuts through the batter.

tagliatelle alla carbonara with prosciutto
Ruth Rogers

Serves 4

Ingredients

1 tablespoon extra virgin olive oil

300g (11oz) prosciutto slices, cut
into strips 1cm wide

100g (3½oz) unsalted butter

150ml (5fl oz) white wine

6 egg yolks

50g (2oz) Parmesan, freshly grated,
plus extra for serving

50g (2oz) aged pecorino,
freshly grated

350g (12oz) egg tagliatelle

Method

- Heat the olive oil in a thick-bottomed pan, add two-thirds of the prosciutto and fry very briefly.
- Add half the butter and the wine, then simmer for 2–3 minutes, just to combine the wine with the butter and the prosciutto juices.
- Mix the egg yolks with the cheeses and season.
- Cook the tagliatelle in boiling salted water until al dente, then drain, reserving a few tablespoons of the pasta water.
- Add the pasta to the prosciutto, then stir in the egg mixture, letting the heat of the pasta cook the egg.
- Add the reserved cooking water if the sauce seems too thick.
- Stir in the remaining prosciutto and butter and serve with extra Parmesan.

Wine expert Tim Atkin's choice
Puglia Rosso

This is a classic carbonara, so we have to have an Italian red. This wine is a warm southern red from the boot heel of Italy – Puglia. It is a generously flavoured wine – a pasta-bashing red. It is a fantastic, heady blend – unoaked, so we get masses of fruit flavours. It is quite a rich dish, with the butter, pasta and cheeses, so we need something with acidity and lots and lots of fruit.

fresh crumpets with fried duck egg, mushrooms and pancetta

Marcus Wareing

Serves 4

Ingredients

For the crumpets

7g (¼oz) fresh yeast
275ml (10fl oz) warm water
225g (8oz) plain flour, sifted
7g (¼oz) table salt
light olive oil, for greasing

For the topping

60g (2½oz) unsalted butter
150g (5oz) pancetta, cut into lardons
20 button mushrooms, cut into quarters
1 tablespoon chopped flat-leaf parsley
light olive oil, for frying
4 duck eggs
black pepper, freshly ground
salt

For the dressing

20ml (¾fl oz) red wine vinegar
125ml (4½fl oz) extra virgin olive oil

Method

- Place the yeast in a bowl and whisk in the warm water.
- Place the sifted flour in a separate bowl with the salt and whisk in the yeast mixture until smooth. Cover the bowl with cling film and leave in a warm place for 1 hour to prove, until at least doubled in volume.
- Preheat the oven to 170°C/325°F/Gas Mark 3.
- Heat a fine layer of light olive oil in a non-stick pan over a low to medium heat. Lightly oil the inside of 4 metal chef's rings (9cm diameter/2cm high), then place them in the pan.
- Pour or ladle enough batter into each ring to fill halfway.
- Cook the crumpets on the hob until the top has set. Remove the rings, turn the crumpets over and cook for 1 minute to colour.
- Transfer to a baking tin, place in the centre of the oven and continue to cook for 5 minutes. Remove and cool on a wire rack.
- Preheat the grill to medium.
- Place the vinegar and olive oil in a bowl, whisk together and season.
- Heat a frying pan until hot and add 25g (1oz) of the butter and the pancetta and fry for about 3 minutes until crispy.
- Add the mushrooms, season and fry for a further 3–4 minutes until golden-brown. Finish with the chopped parsley and a grind of pepper.
- Meanwhile, heat a second frying pan until hot and add a little oil.
- Crack the eggs into the pan, making sure that the yolks are in the centre, and cook gently until the whites are fully cooked.
- Place the pan under the grill for 1 minute to warm the yolks.
- While the eggs are cooking, toast the crumpets until golden-brown.
- Using an 8cm plain-edged pastry cutter, cut the duck eggs into neat rounds and season them with a little black pepper and sea salt.
- Butter the crumpets and place one on each plate with an egg on top.
- Spoon the mushrooms and bacon on top and a drizzle of dressing.

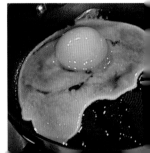

pork escalope with fennel and green bean salad

James Martin

Serves 2

Ingredients

For the pork

1 x 200–225g (7–8oz) pork fillet

25g (1oz) plain flour

1 egg, beaten

3 tablespoons milk or water

110g (4oz) croutons, crushed

25g (1oz) butter

1 tablespoon vegetable oil

For the fennel and green bean salad

1 bulb of fennel, finely sliced

75g (3oz) green beans, finely sliced

8 asparagus tips

2 celery sticks, finely sliced

2 tablespoons extra virgin olive oil

juice of ½ lemon

20g (¾oz) Parmesan, finely grated

1 bunch of parsley, finely chopped

75g (3oz) cooked baby beetroot

Method

- Slice the pork fillet on the diagonal to make 1cm thick slices.
- Season the flour with salt and black pepper.
- Dip the pork into the flour and shake off any excess.
- Season the egg and whisk in the milk or water.
- Dip the pork into the egg mixture and then the crouton crumbs.
- Heat a frying pan until hot and add the butter and oil.
- Add the pork and fry on each side for 2–3 minutes until golden-brown and cooked through.
- To make the salad, toss the fennel, green beans, asparagus tips and celery together.
- Whisk the olive oil, lemon juice and Parmesan together, then season with black pepper. Pour over the salad, add the parsley and toss to combine.
- Serve the pork with a spoonful of salad and the beetroot scattered around the edge.

tagliarini with prosciutto, peas, spring onion and Parmesan

Theo Randall

Serves 4

Ingredients

200g (7oz) Italian '00' flour
1 whole egg
6 egg yolks
50g (2oz) fine semolina flour
50g (2oz) butter
6 spring onions, thinly sliced
200g (7oz) fresh peas, podded
75g (3oz) prosciutto, roughly chopped
50g (2oz) Parmesan, finely grated

Method

- To make the pasta, place the flour, egg and yolks in a food processor and process for 1 minute until everything is bound together.
- Place in a bowl, cover with cling film and place in the fridge to rest for 30 minutes.
- Divide the pasta dough in half, then pass one half through a pasta machine a few times, gradually reducing the thickness, until the pasta feels elastic.
- Add the tagliarini cutter to the pasta machine, pass the pasta through to form thin strips and dust with the semolina flour.
- Repeat the process with the remaining dough and place the pasta in the fridge overnight.
- When you are ready to cook the pasta, bring a large pan of salted water to the boil, then add the tagliarini and cook for 2–3 minutes until tender.
- Meanwhile, heat a frying pan until warm and add the butter and spring onions. Fry for 1 minute until just softened, then add the peas and a splash of water to cover.
- Simmer for 1 minute, then add the prosciutto and cook for a further minute.
- Drain the pasta, place in the pan with the peas and toss to combine.
- Add the Parmesan, season to taste and serve immediately.

Wine expert Olly Smith's choice

Riff Pinot Grigio

This wine gives you an extra lift and is so fresh, it's going to let those peas flourish. It also has a lovely tang to it, which is going to work both with the Parmesan and the spring onions, plus the texture has a little bit of zip, which is going to cut through that prosciutto beautifully.

griddled pork chops with chorizo, wild garlic, potatoes and herb dressing

Jun Tanaka

Serves 4

Ingredients

For the pork chops

4 x 200g (7oz) French-trimmed
   pork chops
1 tablespoon olive oil
salt
black pepper

For the marinade

4 tablespoons tomato puree
2 tablespoons soy sauce
2 tablespoons honey
4 tablespoons red wine vinegar

For the potatoes

1 tablespoon olive oil
200g (7oz) Roosevelt potatoes,
peeled, par-boiled and sliced
200g (7oz) chorizo, thickly sliced
125g (4½oz) wild garlic
125g (4½oz) piquillo peppers,
   finely sliced
1 large pinch of smoked paprika

For the herb dressing

4 tablespoons finely chopped basil
2 tablespoons finely chopped
   flat-leaf parsley
3 tablespoons finely chopped mint
1 tablespoon roughly chopped capers
1 teaspoon Dijon mustard
4 anchovy fillets, roughly chopped
juice of ½ lemon
½ clove garlic, finely chopped
200ml (7fl oz) extra virgin olive oil
1 punnet of basil cress, to garnish

Method

- Preheat the oven to 200°C/400°F/Gas Mark 6.
- Heat a griddle pan until hot.
- Rub the olive oil over the pork chops, season with salt and black pepper, place on the griddle and cook for 1 minute on each side.
- Meanwhile, place all the ingredients for the marinade into a bowl and whisk to combine.
- Spoon over the pork chops and place in the oven for 5 minutes.
- To prepare the potatoes, heat a frying pan until hot and add the olive oil.
- Add the potatoes and fry for 2 minutes, then add the chorizo and cook for a further 2 minutes.
- Add the wild garlic, peppers and paprika and cook for 1 minute.
- Thoroughly combine all the herb dressing ingredients except the basil cress in a bowl.
- To serve, spoon the potatoes and chorizo onto a serving plate, place the pork on top and spoon the dressing around, finishing with a few scattered leaves of basil cress.

Wine expert Peter Richards's choice

Tesco Finest Old Vines Tempranillo

Jun's pork and chorizo dish has lots of delicious rustic and spicy flavours and those two things make me think of Spanish and Italian red wines because they can have that very fresh, bittersweet fruit character.

The tempranillo grape gives us lots of fresh fruit and has a slightly herbal character that makes me think of the basil cress and mint in the dish. The delicious tangy freshness on the palate will go really well with the pork, anchovies and capers, and there is also a lovely spicy lift on the finish to match the paprika.

Best

Poultry & Game

roasted chicken breast with a leek and green bean vinaigrette

Angela Hartnett

Serves 4

Ingredients

For the chicken

4 large corn-fed chicken breasts,
  skin on
2 tablespoons olive oil
salt
black pepper

For the vinaigrette

600g (1lb 5oz) green beans
16 baby leeks
½ teaspoon Dijon mustard
50ml (2fl oz) cider vinegar
250ml (9fl oz) olive oil
2 banana shallots, finely diced
2 teaspoons finely chopped tarragon
4 teaspoons finely chopped
  flat-leaf parsley

Method

- Preheat the oven to 180°C/350°F/Gas Mark 4.
- Season the chicken with salt and black pepper.
- Heat a frying pan until hot and add the olive oil and chicken, skin side down.
- Cook for 2–3 minutes until golden, then turn over and cook for a further minute.
- Place in the oven for 12 minutes until cooked through.
- Remove and rest for a few minutes.
- Meanwhile, bring a large pan of salted water to the boil and add the beans and leeks.
- Cook for 2–3 minutes, then drain and refresh.
- Place the mustard, vinegar and olive oil in a bowl and whisk to combine.
- Slice the beans and leeks into 3 on the diagonal and toss into the dressing.
- Add the shallots and herbs and season to taste.
- Pile onto a serving plate and top with the chicken breasts, each one sliced into 3.
- Drizzle over the extra dressing.

Wine expert Peter Richards's choice

Clos d'Yvigne Bel Ami Rosé

The colour of this wine is almost like that of a red wine – deep and luscious – and that tells me that this is going to be full bodied. We've got that lovely, ripe-fruit nose, but it is also peppery, which is going to tie in well with the vegetables and chicken. On the palate, it's spicy and has a little bit of fresh tang to go with the vinaigrette. This is a wonderful, modern-style rosé to go with this dish.

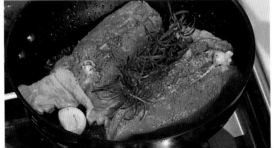

peppered duck with cherries, lovage and elderflower dressing

Lawrence Keogh

Serves 2

Ingredients

2 duck breasts
4 teaspoons crushed black
   peppercorns
1 tablespoon vegetable oil

For the dressing

125g (4½oz) cherries, stoned
50ml (2fl oz) elderflower cordial
50ml (2fl oz) cider vinegar
100ml (3½fl oz) rapeseed oil
salt

For the salad

75g (3oz) bull's blood lettuce
25g (1oz) lovage or celery leaves
½ punnet of mustard cress
25g (1oz) fresh elderflower leaves

Method

- Trim the duck breasts, removing any excess sinew, and score the skin lightly.
- Roll the duck breasts in the crushed peppercorns, then season.
- Heat a frying pan until hot, then add the vegetable oil and duck, skin side down.
- Cook for about 1 minute, then reduce the heat and cook for about 5 minutes on each side for medium-rare breasts that will be nice and pink in the middle.
- Remove the duck from the pan and rest on a wire rack over a plate.
- To prepare the dressing, place the cherries and cordial in a saucepan and bring to a gentle simmer. Do not boil – just let the cherries warm through and bleed their colour into the cordial.
- Remove from the heat and cool.
- Remove the cherries and set aside, then whisk in the cider vinegar and rapeseed oil.
- Add a pinch of salt but no pepper and return the cherries to the pan.
- To serve, place the lettuce leaves, lovage and cress in a bowl and dress with a little of the dressing.
- Cut the duck into thin slices.
- Layer the salad and duck on a plate.
- Spoon some more dressing around the outside of the salad.
- Finish with a sprinkling of the elderflower leaves.

Wine expert Susie Barrie's choice

Porta Reserva Pinot Noir

This has a lingering, refreshing kind of finish that will go well with the sweet, succulent duck meat, but it's also an easy-going wine that will go with the elderflower and even the cider vinegar.

gymkhana chicken pie
Atul Kochhar

Serves 4–6

Ingredients

1 tablespoon coconut or vegetable oil

2 cloves

10 Tellicherry or ordinary black
 peppercorns

1 x 2½cm piece of cassia bark

12 curry leaves

1 teaspoon grated ginger

1 medium onion, cut into 2½cm dice

50g (2oz) plain flour

500g (1lb 2oz) boneless chicken
 thighs, diced

8–12 baby carrots, peeled, blanched
 and cut into 2½cm dice

16–20 silverskin onions

15 green beans cut into 2½cm pieces
 and blanched

2 tablespoons seasoned flour

1 teaspoon turmeric powder

½ teaspoon coriander powder

400ml (14fl oz) coconut milk

110g (4oz) ready-made puff
 pastry sheet

1 egg, beaten, to brush the pastry

For the crust

1 teaspoon coriander seeds

½ teaspoon cumin seeds

1 teaspoon fennel seeds

1 teaspoon black sesame seeds

Method

- Preheat the oven to 200°C/400°F/Gas Mark 6.
- Heat the oil in a large frying pan and sauté the cloves, peppercorns, cassia bark and curry leaves for 1 minute.
- Add the ginger and onion and sauté until translucent.
- Season the flour and toss the chicken thighs in it until they are completely coated.
- Add the chicken thighs to the pan and sauté to seal them, then add the carrots, silverskin onions, beans and spices and cook for 1 minute. Add the seasoned flour and cook for a further 2–3 minutes.
- Add coconut milk and simmer for a further 5–7 minutes, then remove the pan from the heat and leave to cool.
- Spoon the filling into a pie dish until it comes almost to the top.
- Place a pie funnel or an egg cup in the centre of the dish to hold the pastry up as it cooks.
- Roll out the pastry until it is slightly larger than the circumference of the pie dish. Wet the edges of the pastry with water or milk and place it over the dish. Pinch the edges firmly around the rim of the dish to seal the pastry.
- Crush the coriander, cumin, fennel and sesame seeds together into a crust. Brush the top of the pie with the beaten egg and sprinkle the spice crust on top.
- Bake in the preheated oven for 10–12 minutes, or until the pastry is golden-brown and crisp at the edges. Serve with a leafy salad.

Wine expert Olly Smith's choice

Casillero del Diablo Viognier

This wine has a wonderfully syrupy texture to pick up on the coconut in the dish and a bit of spice that is going to go with the savoury nature of the pastry.

chicken breast with lemon and saffron
Gennaro Contaldo

Serves 4

Ingredients

For the chicken
4 chicken breasts, skin on
110ml (4fl oz) extra virgin olive oil
4 large shallots, cut into quarters
2 carrots, julienned
150g (5oz) fresh peas
a few saffron strands, soaked in 5
    tablespoons of warm water
zest of 1 lemon, to garnish
salt
black pepper

For the marinade
3 tablespoons extra virgin olive oil
juice of 3 lemons
175ml (6fl oz) white wine
2 tablespoons white wine vinegar
1 small red chilli, finely chopped
2 bay leaves, roughly torn

Method
- Season the chicken breasts with salt and freshly ground black pepper, rubbing in well.
- Place in a dish together with all the marinade ingredients and mix well.
- Cover the dish and place in the fridge for a couple of hours to marinate, turning the chicken breasts over from time to time.
- Preheat the oven to 180°C/350°F/Gas Mark 4.
- Heat a large frying pan until hot and add 6 tablespoons of the extra virgin olive oil, then add the shallots, carrots and peas and cook on a low heat until softened.
- Remove the vegetables and set them aside.
- Heat the remaining oil in the frying pan, add the chicken breasts and seal on both sides over a high heat.
- Remove from the heat and add the vegetables, then strain the marinade over.
- Place in the preheated oven and bake for 1 hour, or until the chicken is cooked through and the sauce has reduced by half. About 15 minutes before the end of the cooking time, pour in the saffron and its soaking liquid.
- To serve, place the chicken breasts on plates with the vegetables alongside and the sauce spooned over. Sprinkle the lemon zest over the top.

Wine expert Olly Smith's choice
Peconna

This wine has the lift and the citrus zest that is so refreshing. It's like a blast of the cool Adriatic right at you. It's got the elegance to work with the summer vegetables and the verve to work with the tang of the chilli.

roast partridge on a bed of caramelized butternut squash with green herb sauce

Brian Turner

Serves 4

Ingredients

For the partridge and squash

2 tablespoons olive oil

4 grey-legged partridges

2kg (4lb 4oz) butternut squash, peeled

25g (1oz) butter

1 tablespoon runny honey

For the green herb sauce

1 clove garlic, crushed

1 tablespoon chopped parsley

1 tablespoon chopped chervil

1 teaspoon chopped tarragon

1 tablespoon chopped capers

1 tablespoon chopped gherkins

2 anchovy fillets, chopped

1 teaspoon Dijon mustard

2 tablespoons white wine vinegar

8 tablespoons olive oil

Method

- Preheat the oven to 200°C/400°F/Gas Mark 6.
- Heat a large frying pan until hot and add the olive oil and cook the partridges on each side until golden-brown.
- Place in the oven to roast for about 20–25 minutes, depending on size.
- Cut the butternut squash in half lengthways and remove the seeds. Then cut each half lengthways into 4 even-sized pieces.
- Place the butter and honey in a small saucepan and heat until melted.
- Brush over the squash, then place on a baking tray and roast in the oven for 10–15 minutes until tender.
- Remove the partridges from the oven and rest for 10 minutes.
- To make the sauce, place the garlic and herbs in a bowl.
- Add the capers, gherkins and anchovies, then stir in the mustard, vinegar and olive oil.
- Stir to combine and season to taste.
- To serve, place some squash on each plate, then top with the partridge. Pour some of the sauce over and serve the rest separately.

Wine expert Olly Smith's choice

Château Musar, Gaston Hochar

I am looking for a red wine with enough richness and spice to complement the gamey flavours in this dish. This wine from Lebanon has just the right amount of acidity for the gherkins and capers. It's got lovely fruit that is going to work so well with the honey and the butternut squash, and it's got the perfect rustic quality that is going to big-up Brian's tasty birds.

Zanzibar chicken – kuku aku paka

Paul Merrett

Serves 4

Ingredients

2 tablespoons groundnut oil

1 large chicken, jointed into
   8 pieces

2 onions, finely chopped

3 cloves garlic, crushed

2 green chillies, chopped

3 green or red tomatoes, finely
   chopped

½ teaspoon ground turmeric

½ teaspoon cumin seeds

½ teaspoon coriander seeds

4 cardamom pods

juice of 2 limes

275ml (9fl oz) chicken stock

2 x 400ml (14fl oz) tins coconut milk

1 bunch of basil

cooked basmati rice, to serve

Method

- Heat a deep-sided frying pan until hot and add the oil and then the chicken pieces.
- Fry for 1 minute on each side to colour, then transfer to a plate and set aside.
- Add the onions, garlic, one of the chillies and the tomatoes to the pan and cook for 5 minutes.
- Meanwhile, place the turmeric, cumin, coriander and cardamom in a pestle and mortar and grind until fine, then add to the onion and tomato mix along with the lime juice.
- Add the chicken stock and coconut milk and bring to the boil.
- Return the chicken to the pan and simmer for 20 minutes, until the chicken is cooked through.
- Place the remaining chilli and the basil in a pestle and mortar and grind to a paste.
- Add to the chicken at the last minute and season to taste.
- Serve with basmati rice.

Wine expert Olly Smith's choice

Ken Forrester Handmade Chenin Blanc

I'm looking for a wine with enough texture to cope with the coconut and enough of an aromatic quality to look to the spice. For too long this grape variety has been overlooked in the nation's shops. It works super well with lighter curries. It can produce wines that are very zesty or quite sugary, but this wine has the best of both worlds. It is not going to swamp the delicate, perfumed flavours and spices in this dish.

chorizo and brandy chicken

Dave Myers

Serves 4

Ingredients

For the chicken

2 tablespoons vegetable oil

1 chicken, jointed

570ml (1 pint) chicken stock

1 onion, peeled and quartered

2 cloves

1 large carrot, halved

1 celery stick, halved

2 bay leaves

a few sprigs of fresh thyme

1 teaspoon smoked paprika

4 cloves garlic, skin on, slightly bruised

For the sauce

1 tablespoon plain flour

1 tablespoon unsalted butter

4 tablespoons brandy

110g (4oz) cured chorizo sausage, finely chopped

110g (4oz) Manchego cheese, grated (or Parmesan if not available)

To serve

4 jacket potatoes, baked

225g (8oz) green beans, cooked

Method

- In a frying pan, heat the oil over a medium heat and cook the chicken portions for about 5–6 minutes, turning frequently, until browned all over.
- In a large saucepan, bring the stock to the boil.
- Stud one of the onion quarters with the two cloves and add all the onion to the pan along with the chicken, carrot, celery, bay leaves, thyme, paprika and garlic.
- Simmer very gently, uncovered, for 30–45 minutes, until the chicken just starts to fall apart.
- Remove the chicken and place in a roasting tin.
- Strain the stock through a sieve into a bowl and set aside.
- Preheat the oven to 180°C/350°F/Gas Mark 4.
- To make the sauce, place the reserved stock in a saucepan, bring to the boil, then reduce the heat and simmer until the liquid has reduced by half.
- In a bowl, blend the flour and butter together to form a paste (a beurre manié).
- Whisk this paste into the stock along with the brandy and simmer for 3–4 minutes until the sauce has thickened.
- Add the chorizo and season to taste.
- Pour this sauce over the chicken, sprinkle over the grated cheese and place in the oven for 10–15 minutes.
- Serve with the jacket potatoes and green beans.

Wine expert Olly Smith's choice

La Riada Old Vines Garnacha

I'm going to choose this red from the lighter end of the spectrum. It has a little whiff of spice to it which is going to pick up brilliantly on the chorizo and paprika. Light, fruity and with a bit of a kick, this wine has real character.

honey-roasted duck with wild mushroom fricassée, tarragon and spinach

Michael Caines

Serves 4

Ingredients

For the duck

4 x 175g (6oz) duck breasts

1 tablespoon vegetable oil

4 tablespoons clear honey

2 teaspoons Chinese five-spice

salt

black pepper

For the fricassée and spinach

110g (4oz) unsalted butter

1 shallot, finely chopped

150g (5oz) wild mushrooms

1 tablespoon lemon juice

75ml (3fl oz) water

1 tablespoon finely chopped tarragon

200g (7oz) baby spinach

salt

black pepper

Method

- Refrigerate the duck breasts well before attempting to score the skins (you could pop them in the freezer for a few minutes). Score the fatty skin in a criss-cross manner with a very sharp knife, but be careful not to cut the meat. Season with salt and pepper.
- Heat the vegetable oil in a large, flat-bottomed pan and add the breasts, skin side down. Cook at a fairly high temperature, so that the skin renders, but be careful not to burn.
- Once the skin is golden-brown and crisp, turn the breasts over and seal the other side for 1 minute before turning them over once more.
- Turn the heat down slightly and cook for 5–8 minutes.
- Meanwhile, mix the honey and Chinese five-spice together.
- When the duck is cooked, remove from the pan, brush with the honey and allow to rest.
- To prepare the fricassée, heat a frying pan until medium hot and add 25g (1oz) of the butter, the shallot and a pinch of salt.
- Sweat for 2–3 minutes until transparent. Add the wild mushrooms and lemon juice, cover with a lid and sweat for 1 minute.
- Add the water, bring to the boil and whisk in the remaining butter.
- Season with salt and pepper and then add the tarragon.
- Wilt the spinach in a pan in a little butter or olive oil and season.
- To serve, place some spinach on each plate. Slice the duck breasts in half lengthways, place one on top of the spinach on each plate and spoon some of the mushroom fricassée around.

Wine expert Susie Barrie's choice

This is quite a light wine, but it's got loads of lovely red-berry fruit, which is going to be perfect for this Cantonese-style dish.

chargrilled breast of pheasant with creamed Brussels sprouts, chestnuts and smoked bacon

Stuart Gillies

Serves 2

Ingredients

110g (4oz) chestnuts

2 pheasant breasts, boneless

2 pheasant thighs, boneless

2 tablespoons olive oil

200g (7oz) smoked bacon lardons

250g (9oz) Brussels sprouts, finely shredded

400ml (14fl oz) double cream

150ml (5fl oz) red wine

Method

· Preheat the oven to 200°C/400°F/Gas Mark 6.

· Using a sharp knife, cut a cross into the bottom of each chestnut.

· Place on a baking tin and place in the oven for 20 minutes until tender.

· Allow to cool, then peel off the shells, slice finely and set aside.

· Season the pheasant and lightly drizzle with the olive oil.

· Heat a griddle pan until hot, add the pheasant pieces, skin side down, and lightly griddle until golden-brown.

· Turn the pieces over and continue to griddle them until they are almost cooked but still a little pink.

· Meanwhile, heat a frying pan until hot, then add the bacon and fry until golden-brown.

· Drain off the fat and place the bacon in a saucepan with the chestnuts, sprouts and cream.

· Bring to the boil and cook for about 4 minutes, until the sprouts are just tender and the cream is reduced.

· Bring the red wine to the boil in a small frying pan and cook until reduced by two-thirds.

· To serve, place the sprout and chestnut mixture on two warm plates, top with a breast and thigh and spoon the red wine reduction around.

Wine expert Susie Barrie's choice

Walker's Pass Zinfandel

This wine has a gorgeous creaminess that is going to go so well with the sprouts, chestnuts and bacon. But this wine is also very raisiny, rich and fruity, and these flavours are going to be fantastic with the griddled pheasant and the slightly punchy flavour of the sprouts.

country captain chicken curry

Atul Kochhar

Serves 4

Ingredients

1 large roasting chicken, cut into
   8 pieces, skin on

125g (4½oz) butter

3 large onions, thinly sliced

2 cloves garlic, minced

1 tablespoon grated fresh ginger root

2 cloves, bruised

2 bay leaves

1 x 2½cm cassia stick

1 teaspoon turmeric

2 teaspoons ground black pepper

¾ tablespoon finely chopped green
   or red chilli

200ml (7fl oz) chicken stock

juice of ½ lemon

coriander leaves, chopped to garnish

boiled rice, to serve

Method

- Heat a large frying pan until hot, then add half the butter and the chicken pieces.
- Fry on all sides until light brown in colour, then remove and set aside.
- Heat another large frying pan until hot, then add the remaining butter.
- Add the sliced onion and fry until light golden-brown in colour.
- Add the garlic and ginger and fry for 1 minute.
- Add the cloves, bay leaves, cassia, turmeric, black pepper and chillies.
- Fry for 1–2 minutes, then add the chicken pieces and half the stock.
- Reduce the heat and simmer for about 20 minutes until meat is tender. If necessary, add more stock during cooking to prevent the chicken sticking to the pan.
- Add lemon juice and season to taste.
- Garnish with chopped coriander leaves.
- Serve accompanied with boiled rice. You can garnish the dish with red onions cut into rings, crispy shredded bacon, grated coconut, roasted peanuts and chopped hard-boiled eggs.

Wine expert Susy Atkin's choice

De Bortoli Semillon Chardonnay

Atul has put loads of really distinctive flavours into his dish, which calls for a chardonnay, and I think this one has the power and the juiciness to stand up to his recipe. There is a lot of colour and aroma, and bright, juicy flavours in it – lovely peaches and pineapples and wonderful fruity perfumes. We need this to stand up to a dish which has chillies, ginger and chicken.

duck with pomegranate and sautéed escarole – anatra con melagrana

Gennaro Contaldo

Serves 4

Ingredients

For the duck

4 duck breasts, skinless

110g (4oz) plain flour

40g (1½oz) butter

4 tablespoons olive oil

4 pomegranates

For the escarole

1 escarole, cleaned and leaves
   separated

5 tablespoons olive oil

3 cloves garlic, finely chopped

salt

Method

· Preheat the oven to 200°C/400°F/Gas Mark 6.

· Season the duck breasts and dust with the flour, shaking off any excess.

· Heat the butter and olive oil in a large frying pan until the butter begins to foam, then add the duck breasts and seal on each side.

· Place in the oven for 5–6 minutes until just cooked. The duck should be rare.

· Meanwhile, rub two of the whole pomegranates firmly along a surface using the palm of your hand, then cut them in half and squeeze out the juice, as you would with a lemon, all over the cooked duck while it is still in the pan.

· Open the remaining pomegranates, scoop out the seeds and sprinkle them over the duck.

· Place the duck on a plate, pour over the juices from the pan and let it rest for 2–3 minutes before slicing it on the diagonal.

· To prepare the escarole, blanch the leaves for a couple of minutes in boiling salted water, then drain and set aside.

· Heat the olive oil in a pan with a lid, add the garlic and sweat until soft, then add the escarole and gently sauté for 1–2 minutes.

· Reduce the heat, cover and cook for a further 5 minutes, or until the escarole is tender.

· To serve, place some of the escarole on each plate with a few slices of duck and spoon the duck juices over.

Wine expert Olly Smith's choice

This wine is the classic of all classics. It's got flavours that are lasting and really complex. It is going to go brilliantly with the earthy quality of the escarole.

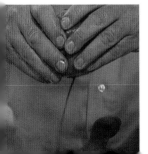

Spiced poussins with coconut cream and rojak salad – ayam golek

Tom Kime

Serves 4

Ingredients

For the poussins

4 poussins

4 dried chillies, soaked in hot water
  to soften

5 shallots, roughly chopped

2 cloves garlic

2cm piece of fresh root ginger

2cm piece of galangal (or ginger)

1 teaspoon salt

4 lemon grass stalks, tough outer
  leaves discarded

300ml (11fl oz) coconut cream

2 teaspoons sugar

juice of 2 limes

For the dressing

2 tablespoons shrimp paste

3 fresh red chillies, deseeded
  and finely chopped

4cm piece of fresh ginger, grated

1 tablespoon mashed tamarind pulp

juice of 1 lime

5 tablespoons boiling water

2 tablespoons fish sauce

3 tablespoons caster sugar

For the rojak salad

½ small cucumber, cut into chunks

¼ fresh pineapple, diced

1 firm, unripe mango, cut into wedges

1 firm, unripe papaya, julienned

1 Granny Smith apple, cut into wedges

2 spring onions, finely sliced

½ bunch of fresh mint leaves, torn

100g (3½oz) blanched roasted
  peanuts, coarsely crushed

Method

· Preheat the oven to 200°C/400°F/Gas Mark 6 and a griddle pan until hot.

· To prepare the poussins, drain the dried chillies once soft. Blend with the shallots, garlic, ginger, galangal and salt (hardest ingredients first), adding a little water if necessary to form a smooth paste.

· Bruise the lemon grass stalks with a rolling pin and place one in the cavity of each poussin. Rub some spice paste over both the insides and outsides of the poussins.

· Put the remaining spice mixture in a pan with the coconut cream and sugar. Bring to a boil, then reduce the heat and simmer until reduced by half.

· Place the poussins on the preheated griddle and cook for 3–4 minutes in total, turning so all sides are sealed.

· Transfer to an oven tin and roast in the oven for 15–20 minutes, basting the chicken with the coconut mixture every 5 minutes, until the chicken is tender and the coconut spice mixture is all used up.

· Remove the poussins and leave to rest in a warm place for 5 minutes. Before serving, pour all the juices in the pan over the chicken and finish with the lime juice.

· Meanwhile, prepare the dressing. Reduce the oven temperature to 180°C/350°F/Gas Mark 4.

· Wrap the shrimp paste in foil and bake for 10 minutes, until it becomes nuttier, drier and aromatic rather than pungent. Grind the chillies and ginger together using a pestle and mortar, then mix in the roasted prawn paste and grind into a pulp. Add the tamarind, lime juice, water, fish sauce and sugar and combine.

· To make the salad, place the cucumber, pineapple, mango, papaya and apple in a bowl and toss together. Add the spring onions and mint, toss gently to combine, then scatter over half the peanuts and stir. Pour the dressing over the salad and stir through.

· To serve, garnish with the salad and the remaining peanuts and mint.

Wine expert Peter Richards's choice

Wakefield Reisling

The great thing about all excellent Australian Reislings is that you get that really lovely, citric lime character which is going to be really refreshing with the dish.

chicken goujons with home-made tomato ketchup

James Martin

Serves 4

Ingredients

For the tomato ketchup

250ml (9fl oz) cider vinegar
1 bay leaf
½ teaspoon ground coriander
½ teaspoon ground cinnamon
8 tablespoons demerara sugar
1½kg (3lb) ripe tomatoes, net weight
   after quartering and seeding
1 teaspoon salt
1 tablespoon English mustard powder
1 clove garlic, crushed
a few drops of Tabasco sauce
2 tablespoons tomato purée
cornflour (if needed)

For the chicken goujons

125g (4½oz) fresh fine breadcrumbs
½ teaspoon cayenne pepper
4 boneless, skinless chicken breasts,
   cut into strips
50g (2oz) plain flour
3 medium eggs, beaten

Method

- To make the ketchup, place the vinegar, spices and demerara sugar in a heavy-based pan and bring to a simmer.
- Add the tomatoes and all the other ingredients and bring to the boil, stirring to prevent any sticking.
- Once up to the boil, reduce the temperature and simmer, stirring most of the time for 30 minutes. Be careful the mix doesn't burn and catch on the base of the pan.
- Blitz in a food processor or liquidizer, push through a sieve and leave to cool.
- If you find the sauce too thin once it is cold, simply re-boil and thicken with a little cornflour mixed to a paste with water, being careful not to make it too starchy and thick. This will prevent the tomato water separating from the sauce.
- To prepare the goujons, heat a deep-fat fryer to 190°C/375°F/Gas Mark 5.
- Mix the breadcrumbs with the cayenne pepper and leave to one side.
- Coat the chicken in flour, then the beaten egg and finally the crumbs, a few pieces at a time, making sure all the chicken is thoroughly coated in each.
- Place a few goujons in the fryer at a time and cook for about 2–3 minutes, until crisp and golden-brown.
- Once cooked, remove onto some kitchen paper to soak up the excess oil.
- Serve with a bowl of the tomato ketchup.

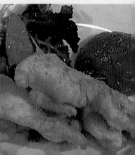

Oriental-style chicken with guacamole

Galton Blackiston

Serves 4

Ingredients

For the marinade

4 tablespoons olive oil

2 tablespoons sesame oil

juice of 1 lime

3cm piece of fresh ginger, peeled and
   finely chopped

2 red chillies, finely chopped

1 bunch of coriander, leaves picked
   and roughly chopped

2 tablespoons soy sauce

2 tablespoons honey

1 tablespoon Worcestershire sauce

For the guacamole

2 ripe avocados, skinned and chopped

juice of 2 limes

1 clove garlic, crushed to a paste

4 tablespoons chopped coriander

1 red chilli, finely chopped

1 shallot, finely chopped

150 ml (5fl oz) olive oil

a splash of Tabasco

For the chicken

4 boneless, skinless chicken breasts,
   cut into 1cm strips

6 spring onions, sliced on the diagonal

2 tablespoons sesame seeds, toasted

Method

· Place all the marinade ingredients in a bowl and mix to combine.
· Add the chicken, stir well and leave to marinate for at least 1 hour.
· Meanwhile, preheat the oven to 200°C/400°F/Gas Mark 6.
· To prepare the guacamole, place the chopped avocados in a bowl and add the lime juice.
· Add the remaining ingredients, mix well and season to taste.
· Heat a griddle pan until hot, then sear the chicken strips for 1–2 minutes, turning once so that they are brown on both sides.
· Transfer the chicken strips to a baking sheet and place in the oven for a further 5 minutes.
· Remove from the oven and season with coarse sea salt and freshly ground black pepper.
· Sprinkle the spring onions and toasted sesame seeds over the chicken and serve with the guacamole.

Wine expert Peter Richards's choice

Saint Clair Vicar's Choice Sauvignon Blanc

This is quite a challenging dish to match a wine to, as it is an amazing Mexican–Asian hybrid thing.

The first things you notice about a good New Zealand sauvignon blanc are those lovely aromatics. They immediately make me think of the coriander, onion and citrus in this dish. This wine has lots of lovely freshness, density and concentration, which means it's going to be able to stand up to the fuller flavours of the soy, chicken and honey.

When buying sauvignon blanc try to spend just a little more than you would usually – you will get wines that are denser, tighter and much more food-friendly as a result.

pan-fried chicken breast with Jerusalem artichoke risotto and roasted vegetables

Mark Sargeant

Serves 2

Ingredients

For the chicken

1 Label Anglaise chicken, legs removed
1 head of garlic
1 bunch of thyme
2 litres (3½ pints) chicken stock
2 tablespoons olive oil
25g (1oz) slightly salted butter
salt
freshly ground pepper

For the risotto

250g (9oz) risotto rice
300g (11oz) Jerusalem artichokes,
    sliced thinly
50g (2oz) butter
50ml (2fl oz) double cream
4 tablespoons freshly grated Parmesan
1 bunch of chives, finely chopped

For the vegetables

200g (7oz) chantenay carrots
200g (7oz) baby turnips
3 cloves garlic
1 bunch of rosemary
2 tablespoons extra virgin olive oil
2 tablespoons honey
2 tablespoons sherry vinegar
1 small punnet of pea shoots, to garnish

Method

- Place the garlic head and several sprigs of thyme into the cavity of the chicken.
- Season with salt and freshly ground black pepper, then place in a large saucepan or casserole and cover with the chicken stock.
- Bring to the boil, then reduce the heat and poach for 25 minutes.
- Remove the pan from the heat and allow the chicken to cool in the stock.
- Remove the chicken from the pan and pat dry, reserving the chicken stock.
- Remove the breasts from the chicken and season with salt and freshly ground black pepper.
- Heat a frying pan until hot and add the olive oil then the chicken, skin side down.
- Fry until the skin is golden-brown, then turn the breasts over, add the butter to the pan and continue to fry until the chicken is cooked through.
- To prepare the risotto, place 500ml (18fl oz) of the stock used to poach the chicken in a saucepan and bring to the boil.
- Add the risotto rice and simmer for 4–5 minutes.
- Drain, discarding the stock, and leave the rice to cool in the saucepan.
- Place the artichokes and half the butter in another saucepan and gently sweat, without colouring, until tender.
- Add the cream and 175ml (6fl oz) of the chicken poaching stock and bring to the boil.
- Pour the artichokes and stock into a blender or processor and blend until a purée is formed.
- Heat the remaining chicken poaching stock back up.

- Place the saucepan of rice back onto the heat and add a ladle at a time of the stock until the rice is tender.
- Add a large spoonful of the artichoke purée, the remaining butter and the Parmesan and stir to combine.
- Stir in the chives.
- Meanwhile, prepare the vegetables. Place the carrots, turnips, two of the garlic cloves and some of the rosemary in a saucepan and cover with water.
- Season and bring to the boil.
- Simmer for 8–10 minutes until tender.
- Drain and pat the vegetables dry.
- Heat a frying pan until hot, then add the olive oil, a little more rosemary and another garlic clove.
- Add the vegetables and fry until golden-brown.
- Add the honey to the pan and deglaze with the sherry vinegar, mixing all the ingredients well.
- To serve, spoon some of the risotto onto the side of each plate and place a chicken breast on top.
- Arrange some of the vegetables on the other side of each plate, top with some pea shoots and drizzle some olive oil around.

Wine expert Olly Smith's choice

Huber Grüner Veltliner

This wine is like Freddie Flintoff – he can bowl, he can bat, he can lead and this bad boy will go with the chicken, the rice and even the artichoke. This wine smells and tastes of white pepper and has a little bit of an aromatic quality along with a herbal edge which is going to work beautifully with the chives and the rosemary.

Best

Fish & Seafood

sea bass with lime and lemon grass

Tom Aikens

Serves 4

Ingredients

For the sea bass
zest of 1 lime
50ml (2fl oz) olive oil
1 teaspoon roughly chopped chervil
1 teaspoon roughly chopped dill
1 teaspoon roughly chopped tarragon
2 medium sea bass fillets, cut into
    12 thin slices

For the lime syrup
zest and juice of 5 limes
40g (1½oz) caster sugar

For the apple and lime purée
3 Braeburn or Granny Smith apples,
    peeled, cored and cut into 1cm
    cubes
zest and juice of 3 limes
15g (½oz) caster sugar

For the lemon grass sauce
500ml (18fl oz) fish stock
500ml (18fl oz) double cream
6 lemon grass stalks, bashed and
    finely chopped
juice of 2 lemons

Method

- Preheat the oven to 200°C/400°F/Gas Mark 6 and place a baking sheet in it.
- Cut four pieces of greaseproof paper large enough to hold three pieces of sea bass each. Rub them with oil and a sprinkle of lime zest.
- Mix the herbs together and divide the mixture into two. Sprinkle half the mixture onto the sheets, place three pieces of fish on each and season.
- For the lime syrup, place the lime zest and juice in a small pan. Add 100ml (3¾fl oz) water and the sugar, bring to the boil and cook to reduce by two-thirds, to form a thick syrup. Leave to cool.
- For the purée, place the apples, lime zest and juice and sugar in a pan. Cook on a low heat, covered, for 8–10 minutes until soft.
- Purée in a blender, then pass through a fine sieve.
- For the lemon grass sauce, place the fish stock in a pan, bring to the boil and cook until reduced by half.
- Add the cream and four of the lemon grass stalks. Reduce by two-thirds.
- Place in a blender, add the remaining lemon grass and purée, then pass through a fine sieve into a small pan.
- Add the lemon juice and season to taste.
- Lift the sheets of paper with the bass on them onto the preheated tray in the oven. Bake for about 2 minutes or until cooked through.
- To serve, place three pieces of bass on each plate. Add some apple purée and drizzle the lime syrup alongside. Froth the lemon grass sauce with a hand blender, then spoon this around. Sprinkle the remaining herbs over.

Wine expert Olly Smith's choice

Tesco Finest Tingleup Riesling

This zesty wine is going to work beautifully with the zip of the apples and the chervil, dill and tarragon in this dish.

chargrilled tuna with red onion, tomato, coriander vinaigrette and shoestring potatoes

Paul Rankin

Serves 4

Ingredients

For the salad

6 plum tomatoes, peeled and cut
   into quarters
2 red onions, roughly sliced
2 tablespoons light olive oil
1 teaspoon coriander seeds, crushed
½ teaspoon salt
125ml (4½fl oz) extra virgin olive oil
2 tablespoons lemon juice

For the tuna

4 x 175g (6oz) tuna steaks
1 tablespoon coriander seeds,
   crushed
1 tablespoon black peppercorns,
   cracked
2 tablespoons light olive oil

For the shoestring potatoes

2 large baking potatoes, finely
   julienned

To serve

2 tablespoons roughly chopped
   coriander
125g (4½oz) rocket leaves

Method

- Preheat the grill to high.
- Toss together the tomatoes, onions, oil, coriander seeds and salt.
- Spread the mixture on a baking sheet and grill for 10 minutes, turning occasionally.
- Transfer to a large bowl, add the extra virgin olive oil and lemon juice, toss to combine and set aside.
- To prepare the tuna, preheat a griddle pan until hot.
- Season the tuna lightly with salt.
- Mix the crushed coriander seeds and cracked peppercorns together and press onto the tuna steaks, making sure that both sides are evenly coated.
- Drizzle with the olive oil.
- Place on the griddle pan and grill for 1–2 minutes on each side.
- To prepare the potatoes, preheat a deep-fat fryer to 190°C/375°F.
- Place the julienned potatoes in a bowl of cold water and soak for 5 minutes, then remove and pat dry.
- Place in the fryer and cook for 2–3 minutes until golden and crispy.
- Drain on kitchen paper and season with salt and black pepper.
- To serve, add the chopped coriander to the tomatoes and onions and spoon some on to each warmed plate. Place a pile of rocket leaves in the centre of each plate and top with a tuna steak cut in half and a pile of shoestring potatoes.

Wine expert Peter Richards's choice

Oyster Bay Merlot Rosé

This wine has a lot of red wine character to it which is necessary to cut through those full flavours of the chargrilled meaty tuna.

squid ink pasta, mussels, saffron and spinach
John Burton Race

Serves 4

Ingredients

2 eggs

3 eggs yolks

3 sachets of squid ink

250g (9oz) Italian '00' flour, plus extra for flouring

2 tablespoons olive oil

2 tablespoons fish stock

1 pinch of saffron strands

1½kg (3lb) mussels

50g (2oz) unsalted butter

2 shallots, finely chopped

2 cloves garlic, finely chopped

150ml (5fl oz) dry white wine

60ml (2½fl oz) double cream

200g (7oz) baby leaf spinach

2 tomatoes, skinned, deseeded and diced

salt

Method

- Whisk the eggs, egg yolks and squid ink together in a bowl.
- Place the flour in a food processor, then pour in the egg and squid ink mixture, pulse until a crumbly dough is formed and add 1 tablespoon of the olive oil. You may need to add a little water to get the dough to the right consistency.
- Turn the dough out onto a floured surface and knead until it becomes smooth and elastic. Cover with cling film and place in the fridge to rest.
- Place the fish stock in a saucepan and bring to the boil, then add the saffron, remove from the heat and leave to infuse.
- Wash and scrape the mussels, discarding any open ones.
- Roll the pasta dough out in a pasta machine to ½mm thickness, in whatever shape desired, such as fettuccini, tagliatelle or spaghetti.
- Heat a large pan with a lid until hot, add the butter, shallots and garlic and cook gently to soften. Turn the heat up high, add the wine and bring to the boil. Tip in the mussels and turn them over and over to coat them in the liquid. Cover the pan and allow the mussels to steam until they open. Discard any that remain closed.
- Cook the pasta in rapidly boiling salted water.
- Meanwhile, add the cream, saffron infusion and spinach to the mussels and mix well. Season and add the tomato.
- Drain the pasta, then return it to the pan and drizzle over 1 tablespoon of olive oil to prevent it sticking together.
- To serve, divide the pasta and ladle the mussels and broth over.

Wine expert Olly Smith's choice

Quinta de Simaens Vinho Verde

This young fresh wine has tropicality and body and is going to work perfectly with the dish.

salt cod and borlotti bean salad

Matt Tebbutt

Serves 4

Ingredients

For the cod

450g (1lb) cod fillet, skin on

200g (7oz) rock salt

juice of 1 lemon

For the bean salad

500g (1lb 2oz) fresh or dried
    borlotti beans

2 bay leaves

1 head of garlic, cut in half

1 red chilli

1 celery stick

1 carrot, peeled

1 onion, peeled and cut in half

150g (5oz) broad beans, blanched

125g (4½oz) samphire, blanched

zest and juice of 1 lemon

4 tablespoons extra virgin olive oil

black pepper, freshly ground

To serve

8 slices ciabatta bread, toasted

1 clove garlic

Method

- Place the cod into a shallow dish and cover with the salt. Cover and place in the fridge for 24 hours.
- Scrape away the salt and pat dry.
- Slice the fish very thinly and place on a plate.
- Squeeze over the lemon juice and marinate for 5 minutes.
- Meanwhile, prepare the beans. If using dried borlotti beans, place in a bowl and cover with water. Soak overnight, then drain and rinse the beans a couple of times.
- Place the soaked or fresh borlotti beans in a saucepan along with the bay leaves, garlic, chilli, celery, carrot and onion and cover with water.
- Bring to the boil, then reduce the heat and simmer for 1–1½ hours until the beans are tender but not breaking up.
- Drain the beans and season to taste.
- Add the broad beans, samphire, lemon juice, zest and olive oil and mix well.
- To serve, spoon some of the beans into the centre of each plate. Arrange strips of cod on top, then season with a good grind of black pepper.
- Rub the toasted ciabatta with the garlic clove and serve alongside.

Wine expert Peter Richards's choice

Val do Sosego Albariño

The reason why Albariño is such a good seafood and fish wine is first and foremost that it is refreshing, with lots of lovely fruit in there. But it also has a slightly salty, saline smell to it, almost like the sea breeze. On the palate, you get all that crisp, zingy fruit, which is going to match really nicely with the cod and the lemon and chilli flavours. It is a rich, full, persistent wine which is going to match the lovely texture of the beans.

shrimp ravioli with shrimp and tomato sauce

James Martin

Serves 4

Ingredients

For the pasta dough

225g (8oz) plain flour

2 medium eggs

2 medium egg yolks

olive oil

For the filling

150g (5oz) peeled Morecambe Bay
   shrimps

½ teaspoon roughly chopped chervil

juice of ½ lemon

For the sauce

25g (1oz) butter

1 shallot, finely chopped

110g (4oz) peeled Morecambe Bay
   shrimps

2 tomatoes, deseeded and diced

2 tablespoons chopped flat-leaf parsley

Method

- Place the flour in a bowl, add the eggs and season. Mix well to form a stiff dough. Continue to mix, gradually adding olive oil to form a smooth dough. Once you have achieved the correct consistency, turn the dough out onto a floured surface and knead for 5 minutes. Cover the dough with cling film and rest for 30 minutes.
- Pass through a pasta machine several times, using increasingly fine settings, until you have at least two thin sheets.
- Blend all the filling ingredients in a food processor to a paste.
- Place a sheet of pasta on a floured surface and place spoonfuls of the filling on the sheet at 7½cm intervals. Brush the pasta around the filling portions with water, then place a second sheet of pasta on top.
- Press down around the fillings portions so that you have a series of sealed parcels, then slice the sheet into squares of ravioli. Repeat this process until you have used up all the pasta sheets and filling.
- Bring a large pan of salted water to the boil, then drop the ravioli into the water and simmer for 3–4 minutes until tender. Drain onto a plate.
- Heat a frying pan until hot, then add the butter, shallot and shrimps and sauté for 2–3 minutes. Add the tomatoes and parsley and season.
- Spoon the sauce over the ravioli and serve.

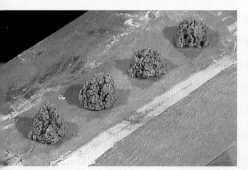

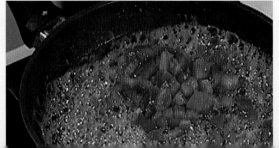

seared hake with crab and crushed potatoes and smoked shrimp sauce

James Tanner

Serves 2

Ingredients

For the hake

1 tablespoon olive oil

2 x 200g (7oz) hake fillets, skin on

salt

black pepper

For the sauce

200g (7oz) smoked shrimps, shells on

1 large shallot, finely chopped

1 leek, white only, finely chopped

2 cloves garlic

2 tablespoons tomato purée

1 tablespoon olive oil

2 tablespoons brandy

225ml (8fl oz) fish stock

125ml (4½fl oz) whipping cream

For the crushed potatoes

250g (9oz) Anya potatoes

110g (4oz) white crab meat

2 plum tomatoes, skinned, deseeded
   and diced

2 spring onions, finely sliced

juice of ½ lemon

1 tablespoon olive oil, plus extra
   for brushing

1 tablespoon chopped dill

salt

Method

- Preheat the oven to 200°C/400°F/Gas Mark 6.
- To prepare the fish, heat a frying pan until hot, then add the olive oil.
- Season the fish with salt and black pepper and place, skin side down, in the frying pan for 1 minute.
- Place in the oven for 4 minutes, then remove and allow to rest.
- De-shell the shrimps and set aside, reserving the shells.
- Heat a deep, non-stick frying pan until hot, add the olive oil, shallot and leek and cook gently for 1 minute, making sure you don't allow them to colour. Add the garlic and sauté for a further minute.
- Add the tomato purée and shrimp shells and cook for 4 minutes.
- Deglaze with the brandy, then add the fish stock and simmer for a further 4 minutes.
- Add the cream and season to taste.
- Place in a blender and blitz until smooth, then pass the mixture through a fine sieve into a clean saucepan.
- Bring to a simmer and add the shelled shrimps.
- To prepare the potatoes, boil them in salted water until tender, then drain well. Crush the potatoes with the back of a fork, then season.
- Add the crab, tomatoes, spring onions, lemon juice, olive oil and dill and mix together.
- To serve, top the potato with the fish, skin side up. Brush the fish with olive oil, add a squeeze of lemon juice and spoon the sauce over.

Wine expert Susy Atkins's choice

Inycon Chardonnay

This wine has just the right note between fresh acidity and rich ripeness for the simple, yet indulgent seafood flavours in this recipe.

cumin-and-sumac-crusted barramundi with avocado hummus

Silvena Rowe

Serves 4

Ingredients

For the barramundi

8 barramundi fillets, bones removed, skin on

2 tablespoons grapeseed oil

3 tablespoons cumin seeds, toasted and crushed

1 teaspoon sumac

2 shallots, peeled and chopped

110ml (4fl oz) dry white wine

2 tablespoons chopped chives

2 tablespoons chopped oregano

For the avocado hummus

2 ripe avocados, peeled, stone removed and cut into cubes

juice of ½ lemon

4–5 tablespoons extra virgin olive oil

3 cloves garlic, crushed

4 tablespoons tahini

2 tablespoons ground cumin

½ teaspoon sumac

1 tablespoon black sesame seeds

Method

- Season both sides of the barramundi fillets, brush with 1 tablespoon of the grapeseed oil, then sprinkle with the cumin and sumac.
- Heat a frying pan until hot, then add the remaining grapeseed oil and the barramundi and cook for about 2 minutes on each side.
- Remove the barramundi from the pan and set aside.
- Add the shallots to the pan and cook for 2–3 minutes, then add the wine and simmer until reduced to less than half.
- Stir in the fresh herbs and season.
- To prepare the hummus, place the avocado cubes in a food processor with the lemon juice and process until smooth.
- Now add the olive oil, garlic, tahini, cumin and sumac and continue to process until the mixture is the consistency of mayonnaise.
- Remove the hummus to a bowl and mix in the sesame seeds.
- To serve, place a couple of barramundi fillets on each plate, drizzle with the white wine and herb sauce and serve with a spoonful of avocado hummus alongside.

Wine expert Susie Barrie's choice

Pazo Serantellos Albariño

Silvena's barramundi is quite a modern style of dish, with its use of Australasian flavours, and probably the best style of wine to go with a fishy fusion dish is a New World riesling. But I fancy something a little bit different, so I'm going to go for a much less well-known style of wine which is fantastic and goes with just about any fish dish you can think of.

It is crisp, dry, elegant, refreshing but restrained and far less punchy than a New World riesling would be. The barramundi is quite a delicately flavoured fish and it's only been dusted in those spices before being pan-fried, so I think that this is going to be a perfect match.

wild salmon with crushed peas and marjoram and vine tomato dressing

Jason Atherton

Serves 2

Ingredients

For the salmon

1 tablespoon olive oil

2 x 150g (5oz) wild salmon fillets

For the crushed peas with majoram

500g (1lb 2oz) fresh peas, podded

1 tablespoon finely chopped marjoram

2 tablespoons butter

For the vine tomato dressing

1 teaspoon Dijon mustard

1 tablespoon white wine vinegar

3 tablespoons extra virgin olive oil

200g (7oz) ripe baby cherry tomatoes

½ teaspoon caster sugar

1 teaspoon cabernet red wine vinegar

seaweed salt

2 sprigs of basil

Method

· Heat a frying pan until hot, then add the olive oil and salmon, skin side down.

· Cook for 3 minutes, then turn over and cook for a further 3 minutes.

· Remove from the heat and rest.

· Meanwhile, bring a saucepan of water to the boil and add the peas.

· Cook for 1–2 minutes, then drain and refresh in iced water.

· Heat a small frying pan until hot then add the peas, marjoram and butter and heat through, crushing lightly with a wooden spoon.

· To prepare the dressing, whisk the mustard, vinegar and olive oil together and season.

· Place in a blender with the tomatoes and sugar, process until puréed, then remove and pass through a sieve into a bowl.

· Add the red wine vinegar and stir well.

· To serve, put a chef's ring in the middle of each plate, spoon in the peas, pressing down well, then remove the ring.

· Place a salmon fillet on top of each pea circle and spoon the sauce around.

· Finish with a sprinkle of seaweed salt and garnish with a sprig of basil.

Wine expert Peter Richards's choice

Kaituna Hills Sauvignon Blanc

This wine has the extra tang and freshness which will go well with the dish. It leaps out of the glass with those fresh, crunchy, green flavours. On the palate, you get all of those lovely tangy notes which will cut really well through that vinaigrette. It also has passionfruit and gooseberry notes which are really refreshing.

pan-fried squid with borlotti beans, chilli, anchovy, parsley and chopped rocket

Theo Randall

Serves 4

Ingredients

For the beans

300g (11oz) borlotti beans

1 sprig of sage

1 red chilli, pricked with a knife

1 clove garlic, cut into quarters

2 tomatoes

3 tablespoons olive oil

1 teaspoon red wine vinegar

salt

black pepper

For the squid

6 fresh, whole squid

1 tablespoon extra virgin olive oil

1 red chilli, deseeded and finely
    chopped

3 anchovy fillets, chopped

juice of ½ lemon

2 tablespoons chopped flat-leaf
    parsley

To serve

1 handful of chopped rocket, dressed
    with olive oil and lemon juice

Method

- If using dried borlotti beans, soak them overnight in plenty of water.
- Drain and place in a large pan with three times the volume of water.
- Add the sage, chilli, garlic and tomatoes. The tomatoes help to break down the outer skin of the beans.
- Bring to the boil and simmer for 1 hour, until the beans are tender.
- Drain off three-quarters of the water and place the beans and the remaining water in a bowl. Remove and discard the chilli and sage.
- Remove the garlic, mash with a fork and stir into the beans and tomatoes.
- Season with salt and black pepper and stir in the olive oil and vinegar.
- To prepare the squid, peel off the wings and outer membranes and remove the heads and intestines. Cut in half lengthways and scrape out the insides with a knife, then wash thoroughly and pat dry.
- Lay the squid flat on a surface, skin side down, and score them with a sharp knife in a criss-cross pattern. Season and rub oil into the skin.
- Place a non-stick pan on a medium heat and add the squid, scored side down. Cook for 1 minute until golden-brown, then turn over. The squid will curl up.
- Add the chilli, anchovy, lemon juice and parsley to the pan.
- Take the squid out of the pan and slice into bite-sized pieces. Return immediately to the pan and toss briefly.
- To serve, place a spoonful of the beans in the centre of each plate. Place a small amount of rocket on top and then the chopped squid.

Wine expert Tim Atkin's choice

Waitrose Manzanilla Sherry

This full-bodied wine is fortified to 17 per cent alcohol, but it does not taste that way. It will work pretty well with the chillies in this dish.

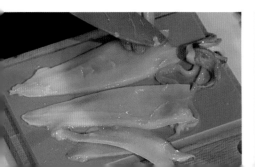

spiced John Dory with mango salsa

Tony Tobin

Serves 4

Ingredients

zest and juice of 1 orange

zest and juice of 1 lemon

1 tablespoon lime marmalade

½ teaspoon ground fennel seeds

½ teaspoon ground cumin

4 x 150g (5oz) John Dory fillets

1 mango, finely diced

1 large tomato, seeded and finely
   diced

1 small red onion, finely diced

1 green chilli, finely sliced into rings

juice of 4 limes

1 tablespoon olive oil

Method

- Place the orange and lemon zests, marmalade and spices in a bowl and mix well to combine. Add some of the orange and lemon juice to make a runny marinade.
- Place the fish on a plate and pour over the marinade, then set aside for 20 minutes.
- Meanwhile, place the mango, tomato, red onion, chilli and lime juice in a separate bowl, mix to combine, season to taste and set aside until the fish is ready.
- Heat a frying pan until hot and add the olive oil and fish, flesh side down.
- Cook for 1–2 minutes on each side until caramelized and cooked through.
- To serve, place some of the salsa in the centre of each plate and top with a John Dory fillet.

Wine expert Tim Atkin's choice

Chapel Down Flint Dry

Not so long ago English wine used to be a bit of a joke, but nowadays, with better winemaking and lots of glorious sunshine, our top wines are more than a match for the best in the world.

I'm going for something that is crisp, elegant and dry and won't compete with the explosion of flavours in this dish. This wine has light body and delicate citrus flavours which will go brilliantly with the John Dory.

grilled turbot on minted cauliflower couscous with walnut, passionfruit and celery salsa

Peter Gordon

Serves 4

Ingredients

For the couscous

125g (4½oz) instant couscous

160ml (5½oz) tepid water

¾ teaspoon salt

225g (8oz) cauliflower florets

1 very large handful of mint leaves

2 tablespoons extra virgin olive oil

For the salsa

1 small red onion, peeled, thinly sliced
 and rinsed in cold water

1 celery stalk, diced

1 tablespoon clementine or satsuma
 juice

seeds and juice of 2 passionfruit

1 handful of flat-leaf parsley, on stalk

a large handful of walnuts, lightly
 toasted and coarsely chopped

2 tablespoons extra virgin olive oil

1 teaspoon soy sauce

2 handfuls of watercress or wild
 rocket, to serve

For the turbot

4 x 150g (5oz) skinless, boneless
 turbot fillets

1 tablespoon olive oil

Method

- To prepare the couscous, mix the couscous with the tepid water and salt in a large bowl and leave it to absorb the water.
- Bring a pot of lightly salted water to the boil and add the cauliflower, making sure it is completely submerged, then boil for 3 minutes until it just begins to soften. Do not overcook it. Alternatively, you can steam it.
- Drain the cauliflower and immediately transfer it to a large bowl of iced water for 2 minutes. Drain it again, then place in a food processor with the mint leaves and olive oil and blitz in several short bursts, scraping any remnants from the side of the processor bowl with a spatula each time, until the mixture is the consistency of coarse crumbs.
- Mix into the couscous and season to taste. It will keep, covered, in the fridge for a day. Give it a mix to loosen it up before serving.
- To prepare the salsa, mix the onion and celery with the citrus juice and the passionfruit and leave to one side.
- Pick some of the smaller leaves from the parsley and shred the rest, stalks and all. Combine with the walnuts in a bowl and set aside.
- Lightly season the fish on both sides and drizzle with the olive oil.
- Heat a griddle pan, then cook the turbot on a moderately high heat for 2–3 minutes on each side, depending on the thickness of the fillets. Turbot should always be served medium-rare (as should all fish), so make sure you don't overcook it. Alternatively, you can cook the turbot under a moderately hot grill. While the fish is cooking, mix the parsley and walnuts with the passionfruit mixture and add the extra virgin olive oil and soy sauce. Season to taste.
- To serve, top the couscous with the watercress or rocket, and a portion of fish on top. Drizzle over any pan juices and spoon the salsa around.

salt-crusted whole sea bass with fennel and rocket salad

James Tanner

Serves 4

Ingredients

For the sea bass

1 sea bass, scaled and gutted
  (about 1.4kg/3lb 2oz)
1 bunch of fresh thyme
4 egg whites
300g (11oz) sea salt
3 tablespoons olive oil
1 lemon

For the fennel salad

1 large fennel bulb, thinly sliced
1 tablespoon chopped dill
juice of 1 orange
3 tablespoons extra virgin olive oil
1 bunch of rocket

For the garlic mash

1 bulb garlic
300ml (11fl oz) whipping cream
500g (1lb 2oz) King Edward potatoes,
cooked and passed through a ricer
75g (3oz) unsalted butter

Method

- Preheat the oven to 200°C/400°F/Gas Mark 6.
- Trim the fins from the sea bass and stuff the gut cavity with the thyme.
- Whisk the egg whites in a bowl until soft peaks form, then fold in the salt.
- Line a baking sheet or ovenproof serving dish with greaseproof paper and spread a third of the egg white mixture over the base.
- Lay the sea bass on top of the egg white mixture, then spoon over the remaining mix, making sure that the fish is completely covered.
- Bake in the oven for 30–35 minutes until crisp.
- Finish by peeling off the salt crust and drizzling with the lemon juice and olive oil.
- To prepare the salad, place the fennel, dill, orange juice and olive oil in a bowl and mix together.
- Leave to stand for 10 minutes, then add the rocket leaves and toss together just before serving.
- To prepare the garlic mash, place the garlic and cream in a saucepan and bring to the boil, then reduce the heat and simmer until the cream is reduced by half.
- Remove the garlic bulb, then mix in the riced potatoes and stir well to combine.
- Add the butter and season to taste.
- To serve, place a spoonful of mash on each plate with the salad alongside and several pieces of sea bass.

bake-in-the-bag monkfish with preserved lemon couscous

Allegra McEvedy

Serves 6

Ingredients

For the monkfish parcels

250g (9oz) couscous

2 teaspoons ground cumin

1 teaspoon cumin seeds

6 spring onions, thinly sliced

2 preserved lemons, sliced and
   roughly chopped

10g (½oz) coriander, roughly chopped

18 cherry tomatoes, quartered

1.2kg (2lb 9oz) monkfish fillet

6 tablespoons extra virgin olive oil

1 teaspoon saffron

2 small fennel bulbs, cut in half, cores
   removed and sliced into 5mm slices

For the salad

1 cucumber, peeled, seeded and
   sliced

15 radishes, sliced thinly

200g (7oz) Greek yoghurt

juice of 1 lemon

½ teaspoon sumac

2 tablespoons extra virgin olive oil

Method

- Preheat the oven to 200°C/400°F/Gas Mark 6.
- Mix all the ingredients for the monkfish parcels except the monkfish, olive oil, saffron and fennel in a bowl and season.
- Lay the monkfish fillet on a chopping board and cut into 1cm thick angled slices. The idea is to have around 2–3 medallions per person.
- Place 180ml (6fl oz) of water in a saucepan, bring to the boil, then add the saffron and remove from the heat.
- Cut out six large sheets of foil and lay them out on a flat surface.
- Pour 2 tablespoons of the olive oil into the couscous and mix well, so that all the grains are well coated, then add the saffron water and mix again.
- Spread a little olive oil in the centre of the front half of each sheet of foil and divide the sliced fennel equally between them, placing it on the oil.
- Divide the couscous equally between the sheets, placing it on the fennel in neat little piles.
- Top each pile of couscous with 2–3 monkfish medallions.
- Drizzle the rest of the oil over the monkfish and season.
- Bring the top edge of one sheet of foil over the fish to meet the bottom edge.
- Line up the side edges and seal them by folding them over three times and pressing down firmly with your fingertips to secure them. Repeat for all the parcels.
- Now the parcels should be well sealed on three sides, with just one side open.

bake-in-the-bag monkfish
with preserved lemon couscous (cont)

Method (cont)

- Carefully place each parcel at a 45 degree angle, so that you are not mucking up the arrangement inside but are able to pour 3 tablespoons of water into each bag without it dribbling out.
- Seal the remaining edge of each parcel with the same neat folds.
- Place the parcels on two baking sheets and pop them into the oven for 15–20 minutes. If the baking sheets are at different heights, swap them around halfway through.
- To prepare the salad, combine all the ingredients in a large bowl and season to taste.
- To serve, place a parcel on each warmed plate, ready to be cut open at the table. Serve the salad in its bowl.

Wine expert Susy Atkins's choice

Montana Unoaked Chardonnay

Allegra's dish has rich ingredients such as saffron and cumin and of course the preserved lemon. I'm going to need a white wine with guts and an assertive flavour.

This chardonnay has a rich aroma and the flavour is ripe and fleshy but without that cloying oaky finish. With the firm, meaty monkfish and the distinctive lemony tang in the dish, this is the perfect wine. It is enough to stand up to all of it, but it won't overpower it.

scallops with mushrooms and a light creamy sauce – coquilles Saint Jacques

Michel Roux

Serves 4

Ingredients

8 scallops, in the shell, well scrubbed
300g (11oz) medium baking potatoes
4 egg yolks
125g (4½oz) butter
200g (7oz) button mushrooms, thinly sliced
juice of ¼ lemon
500ml (18fl oz) fish stock
25g (1oz) plain flour
150ml (5fl oz) double cream
15g (½oz) Gruyère, finely grated
15g (½oz) fine breadcrumbs

For the taboulla

110g (4oz) couscous
110ml (4fl oz) boiling water
1 teaspoon light olive oil
1 head of broccoli

Method

· Lay the scallops on a hotplate for 1–2 minutes until they begin to open (if needed).
· Slide the blade of a filleting knife between the flat side of the shell and the scallop. Then slide the blade between the scallop and the concave side of the shell to detach the scallop and coral.
· Keep the 4 best concave halves for serving. Scrub them under cold water and then dry them out in a very low oven.
· Peel off the membranes surrounding the scallops, clean them in cold water, cut into pieces and keep to one side.
· Separate the whites and corals and wash gently in cold water to eliminate any grains of sand. Drain them and put them in a bowl.
· To make the duchesse potatoes (they can be made the day before and kept in the fridge). Preheat the oven to 220°C/425°F/Gas Mark 7.
· Brush the potatoes under cold running water and prick in 2 or 3 places with the point of a knife.
· Place in the oven on a baking sheet in their jackets for 35–40 minutes, or until soft.
· Slide the point of a knife into the centre of the potatoes to check they are cooked, then halve them, scoop out the insides with a spoon and rub them through a sieve into a bowl.
· Add 2 egg yolks and 25g (1oz) butter and work with a wooden spatula until smooth.
· Season lightly with salt and pepper.
· Fill a piping bag with this mixture and pipe an attractive ribbon around the edge of each concave scallop shell.

scallops with mushrooms
and a light creamy sauce (cont)

- To cook the scallops and mushrooms, put the scallops, corals, membranes, mushrooms and lemon juice in a saucepan with the fish stock, set over a low heat and slowly bring to the boil.
- Lower the heat and simmer very gently at about 80°C/175°F for another minute.
- Take off the heat and put to one side to reach room temperature.
- To make the sauce, melt 50g (2oz) butter in a saucepan, stir in the flour and cook for 2 minutes to make a roux.
- Take the pan off the heat and strain in the stock from the scallops and mushrooms through a conical sieve, stirring all the time.
- Simmer the sauce gently for a few minutes, whisking it frequently.
- In a bowl, mix the remaining egg yolks with the cream, then pour this mixture into the sauce.
- Before it begins to bubble, take the pan off the heat, season the sauce with salt and pepper and keep hot.
  Now assemble the dish. Increase the oven temperature to 240°C/475°F/Gas Mark 9.
- Cut the scallop whites into thick slices.
- Place a layer of mushrooms in each shell, then a layer of scallop whites, then top with the corals.
- Cover generously with sauce and sprinkle the top with a mixture of Gruyère and breadcrumbs.
- Melt the remaining butter and pour it over the top.
- Brown the scallops in the hot oven for 3–5 minutes, until the top of the sauce is lightly glazed and the potato border is pale gold.

- To make the taboulla place the couscous into a bowl and pour the boiling water over it. Season with a little salt and pepper, stir with a fork and cover with cling film for 4–5 minutes.
- Stir again and add the olive oil.
- Shave the very top of the broccoli florets off and add to the couscous.
- Stir gently with a fork and check the seasoning.
- Divide equally between 4 plates, then place the scallops shells on top.
- Serve immediately and do not forget to warn your guests that the dish is extremely hot!

Wine expert Olly Smith's choice

Sainsbury's Taste the Difference Grüner Veltliner

Austrian wine had a bit of a problem in the 80s with the antifreeze scandal, but just like Take That with their massive comeback, Austrian wine is back for good!

This grüner veltliner has subtle flavours of pear and white spices and there is an aromatic quality to it. The texture immediately strikes me. This dish has got mushrooms, Gruyère, potatoes and scallops – they are all big textures but not very big flavours. This wine works because it has substance but not dominant flavours; it is quite subtle.

heaven

Jason Isaacs

Food heaven: pork

'I love every kind of meat and anything spicy. I particularly love pork. I couldn't live without my pork. I could only live in a vegetarian world if it were filled with aubergines.'

Jason was brought up in Liverpool, on a diet of fry-ups. 'We lived in a fried universe. We also used to use the fat from the Sunday roasts as spread for our sandwiches throughout the week in place of butter. My father has since had two quadruple heart bypasses!'

Chinese pork patties on a bed of spring onion, cucumber and coriander with chilli dip

Serves 4

Ingredients

For the patties

1 boneless, skinless chicken breast, roughly chopped

juice of 2 limes

1 teaspoon Chinese five-spice powder

1 tablespoon light soy sauce

400g (14oz) pork mince

1 green chilli, finely chopped

4 tablespoons roughly chopped coriander leaves

2 tablespoons vegetable oil

salt

black pepper, freshly ground

For the dip

2 long red chillies, finely chopped

100g (3½oz) caster sugar

50ml (2fl oz) water

50ml (2fl oz) white wine vinegar

For the salad

juice of 1 lime

3 tablespoons sesame oil

1 teaspoon light soy sauce

4 spring onions, shredded

½ cucumber, shredded

2 tablespoons coriander leaves

Method

- Preheat the oven to 190°C/375°F/Gas 5.
- Place the chicken, lime juice, five-spice powder and soy sauce in a food processor and pulse until just combined.
- Add the pork mince, chilli and coriander and pulse again to combine totally.
- Fry off a little of the mixture to check the seasoning and add salt and freshly ground black pepper to taste.
- Form into balls the size of golf balls and flatten slightly.
- Heat an ovenproof frying pan until hot and add the vegetable oil.
- Fry the patties for 1 minute on each side until coloured, then place in the oven for 4–5 minutes.
- To prepare the dip, place the chillies, sugar, water and vinegar in a saucepan and bring to the boil.
- Cook for 4–5 minutes until just thickened, then cool slightly.
- Meanwhile, prepare the salad by whisking together the lime juice, sesame oil and soy sauce, then tossing with the spring onions, cucumber and coriander leaves.
- To serve, place some salad on each plate, top with a pile of patties and drizzle with the chilli sauce.

Wine expert Tim Atkin's choice
Montana Riesling, Marlborough

Lesley Garrett

Food heaven: gooseberries

'I love gooseberries. My dad would find or catch most of our food and the rest we grew ourselves. We used to grow gooseberries all the time. Together with oily fish, they are just heavenly.

When my dad was a child during the war, he would bunk off school and spend his days catching rabbit and fish. He provided the whole family with delicious fresh produce throughout the war and rationing. He caught a 28-pound pike when he was nine!'

pan-fried mackerel with gooseberry sauce, new potatoes and salad leaves

Serves 2

Ingredients

25g (1oz) butter

250g (9oz) gooseberries, topped
   and tailed

75ml (3fl oz) double cream

1 teaspoon caster sugar

1 mackerel, filleted

1 tablespoon grainy mustard

1 tablespoon olive oil

150g (5oz) new potatoes, scrubbed
   and halved

3 tablespoons extra virgin olive oil

1 bag of salad leaves

Method

· Heat a small pan until hot, then add the butter and gooseberries.
· Cover and simmer for 20–25 minutes until tender.
· Remove the lid and mash the gooseberries down.
· Add the cream and sugar and season.
· Cook for a few minutes.
· Meanwhile, preheat the grill to hot.
· Brush the flesh side of the mackerel fillets with the grainy mustard.
· Brush both sides with olive oil and season.
· Place on a baking sheet, skin side up, and place under the grill for 4–5 minutes until just cooked through.
· Cook the new potatoes until tender, then toss with 1 tablespoon of the extra virgin olive oil and season.
· Toss the salad leaves with the remaining extra virgin olive oil and season.
· To serve, place one mackerel fillet on each plate with a pile of new potatoes, some of the dressed salad and a spoonful of gooseberry sauce.

Wine expert Olly Smith's choice
Wither Hills Sauvignon Blanc

Nigella Lawson

Food heaven: chestnuts

'I really love chestnuts, and they are especially lovely at Christmas time. I love them in a savoury way and also in a Mont Blanc. I do them with pancetta in a stir fry and throw them over some Italian leaves. I think they are just incredible.

My mother was a good cook, the whole family was very passionate about food. My mother believed in child labour and had us around a big stove, all stirring, although the boys never cooked! Very sexist!'

glacéed chestnut and chocolate tart

Serves 8

Ingredients
250g (9oz) glacéed chestnuts

75ml (3fl oz) dark rum

50g (2oz) caster sugar

400g (14oz) good quality chocolate
cake

375g (13oz) dark chocolate, roughly
chopped

200g (7oz) sweetened chestnut purée

560ml (19fl oz) double cream

5 tablespoons cocoa powder

cocoa powder, to serve

Method
- Roughly chop two-thirds of the glacéed chestnuts.
- Place the rum and caster sugar in a saucepan and bring to a simmer, then cook until the sugar has melted.
- Remove from the heat and add the chopped glacéed chestnuts.
- Stir well, then leave to cool.
- Take a 2cm thick round off the top of the chocolate cake and place in the bottom of a 25cm (10in) cake tin.
- Scatter the soaked chestnuts and rum sauce over the chocolate cake.
- Place the chocolate in a bowl over a pan of boiling water and melt.
- Whisk in the sweetened chestnut purée, remove from the heat and allow to cool slightly.
- Pour the cream into the chocolate and chestnut mixture and whisk to combine.
- Pour the mixture over the cake.
- Place in the fridge for at least 2 hours, preferably overnight.
- To serve, dust with cocoa powder and decorate with the remaining glacéed chestnuts.

Wine expert Olly Smith's choice
Quinta do Noval Colheita Tawny Port

Ray Mears

Food heaven: bananas

'Bananas are so undervalued and also so versatile. There is so much you can do with them. When you travel across the tropics, they are just an essential piece of kit.'

Ray has sampled an incredibly diverse range of foods from around the world. He doesn't define foods like witchetty grubs as unusual. 'I don't see foods such as these as bizarre. Processed foods pumped with additives are bizarre.'

banoffee cheesecake with chocolate sauce

Serves 4

Ingredients

For the cheesecake

1 x 225g (8oz) tin condensed milk

150g (5oz) chocolate oat biscuits, crushed

75g (3oz) butter

2 tablespoons honey

4 bananas, peeled and cut into chunks

400g (14oz) cream cheese

4 tablespoons icing sugar

1 tablespoon maple syrup

For the chocolate sauce

40g (1½oz) butter

175ml (6fl oz) double cream

225g (8oz) milk chocolate, roughly chopped

Method

· Place the unopened tin of condensed milk into a saucepan and cover with water.

· Bring to the boil, reduce the heat, cover with a lid and simmer for 1½ hours, topping up the water if necessary.

· Remove the tin from the water and leave to cool.

· Meanwhile, place the crushed biscuits in a bowl, add a third of the butter and the honey and mix together.

· Place four 3-inch ring moulds on a flat plate.

· Spoon the biscuit mixture into each ring mould and flatten with the back of a spoon.

· Heat a frying pan until hot, then add the remaining butter and the bananas and sauté for 2–3 minutes until golden.

· Remove from the pan and set to one side to cool.

· Place the cream cheese and icing sugar in a bowl and whisk until smooth.

· Stir in the maple syrup and the caramelized condensed milk.

· Spoon the mixture on top of the biscuit base in the moulds.

· Place in the fridge for 30 minutes until set.

· To make the chocolate sauce, place the butter and cream in a saucepan and bring to a simmer.

· Add the chopped chocolate and mix to combine.

· Cook until the chocolate is melted and the mixture is smooth and glossy.

· To serve, remove the cheesecakes from the fridge, place one on each plate and remove the ring moulds. Top with some sautéed bananas and a spoonful of chocolate sauce.

Wine expert Peter Richards's choice

Coteaux du Layon Les Chavagnes, Domaine Cady

Charlie Higson

Food heaven: ribs

'I like meat across the board. I love spare ribs, and most American blow-out meat dishes, to be honest.

We grew up in the sixties, with traditional English cooking. My family had no access to fancy ingredients. If you wanted olive oil you had to go to the chemist to get it! I didn't have pasta until I was 12.'

sweet, sticky, spicy ribs with red onion salad

Serves 4–6

Ingredients

For poaching the ribs

1½kg (3lb 4oz) meaty rack of pork
    spare ribs
1 onion, chopped
2 cloves garlic, lightly crushed
½ teaspoon black peppercorns

For the marinade

2 tablespoons olive oil
2 onions, roughly chopped
4 cloves garlic, crushed
2 red chillies, finely chopped
½ teaspoon dried chilli flakes
2 teaspoons crushed fennel seeds
110g (4oz) dark brown sugar
600g (1lb 5oz) tomato ketchup
110ml (4fl oz) dark soy sauce

For the salad

2 red onions, finely sliced
6 tomatoes, cut into chunks
1 small bunch of flat-leaf parsley,
    leaves picked
3 tablespoons extra virgin olive oil
1 tablespoon red wine vinegar

Method

- To poach the ribs, place them in a large, wide saucepan, cover with water and add the onion, garlic and peppercorns.
- Bring to the boil, then reduce the heat, cover and simmer for 1 hour until tender.
- Preheat the oven to 180°C/350°F/Gas mark 4.
- To prepare the marinade, heat a deep-sided frying pan until hot and add the olive oil, onions and garlic.
- Fry for 4–5 minutes until softened.
- Add the chillies, chilli flakes, fennel seeds and brown sugar and cook for a further 1–2 minutes until the sugar has melted.
- Add the tomato ketchup and soy sauce and bring to the boil, then reduce the heat and simmer for 10 minutes until thickened.
- Remove from the heat and allow to cool slightly, then transfer to a food processor and blend until smooth.
- Remove the ribs from the poaching liquor and place on a baking sheet, then coat the ribs with the sticky sauce, making sure they are completely covered.
- Place in the oven for 15 minutes, or until they are sticky and heated through.
- To prepare the salad, place the red onion, tomatoes and parsley leaves in a bowl.
- In a separate bowl, whisk the olive oil and vinegar together, then pour over the salad, season to taste and toss to combine.
- To serve, slice the pork rack into individual ribs and serve with a spoonful of salad alongside.

Wine expert Olly Smith's choice
Mount Langi Ghiran 'Billi Billi Creek' Shiraz

Ronnie Corbett

Food heaven: french beans

'French beans are my all-time favourite vegetables.'

Ronnie brought his own loaf of bread with him when he came on the show. 'My dad was a baker for 28 years. He used to go to work at 10 at night and come back in at 7.30 a.m in the morning. It was a very hard life and he was determined I would go into something else, but I do love baking.'

pickled French beans with mackerel, bacon and taleggio jacket potatoes

Serves 4

Ingredients

For the beans

1 tablespoon olive oil

5 shallots, peeled and finely sliced

2 sprigs of thyme, leaves picked

1 bay leaf

2 cloves garlic, peeled and crushed

1 x 2½cm piece of ginger, finely chopped

2 teaspoons pink peppercorns, crushed

450ml (16fl oz) white wine vinegar

500g (1lb 2oz) French beans, trimmed

75g (3oz) sugar

For the jacket potatoes

4 baking potatoes

8 rashers smoked streaky bacon, cut into lardons

4 small smoked mackerel fillets, skinned, boned and flaked

4 tablespoons crème fraîche

300g (10½oz) taleggio cheese, cut into 4 equal slices

Method

- For the beans, place a thick-bottomed saucepan on a medium heat, add the olive oil, shallots, thyme, bay leaf, garlic, ginger and peppercorns and sweat for 2–3 minutes, without colouring, until soft.
- Add the vinegar to the pan, swirl to combine, then remove from the heat and set aside to cool.
- Meanwhile, bring a pan of lightly salted water to the boil, cook the beans for 2 minutes, then drain and refresh the beans in cold water.
- Toss the beans with the sugar, then pour the cooled vinegar solution over them and set aside.
- For the jacket potatoes, preheat the oven to 200°C/400°F/Gas mark 6.
- Pierce the baking potatoes several times with a knife and place in the oven for 1 hour, until crispy on the outside but tender when pierced with a knife. Remove from the oven and set aside to cool.
- Preheat the grill to high.
- Meanwhile, heat a frying pan until hot, then add the bacon and fry for 3–4 minutes until golden and crispy. Remove the bacon from the pan and set aside to drain on kitchen paper.
- When the potatoes are cool, place them on a board and slice the tops off. Use a spoon to scoop the potato from the skins and place in a bowl.
- Mash until smooth, then mix in the cooked bacon, flaked mackerel and crème fraîche and season to taste.
- Carefully spoon the potato mixture back into the skins and place on a baking sheet.
- Top each with a piece of taleggio cheese and place under the hot grill until golden and bubbling.
- To serve, place a jacket potato on each plate with a spoonful of the pickled French beans.

Wine expert Peter Richards's choice
Argento Chardonnay

Jason Donovan

Food heaven: steak

'I love fillet steak – done any way, really. I'm not a massive overeater of meat, but I crave it and eat it occasionally. My dad brought me up. He and my grandparents are originally from England, so he cooked stuff like egg and chips and roasts. It was only when I was 11 or 12 and my father married my stepmother that my tastes started to dramatically expand. Her cooking was phenomenal. I remember this amazing salmon mousse with melba toast that she used to make.'

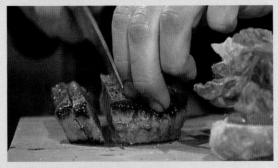

Steak sandwich with caramelized red onions and home-made stout mustard

Serves 4

Ingredients

For the mustard

50g (2oz) white mustard seeds

50g (2oz) black mustard seeds

75g (3oz) soft light brown sugar

2 teaspoons ground allspice

1 pinch of ground cinnamon

1 teaspoon coarse salt

1 teaspoon peppercorns

1 teaspoon paprika

½ teaspoon ground turmeric

125ml (4½fl oz) red wine vinegar

3 tablespoons stout

For the onions

1 tablespoon butter

1 tablespoon olive oil

2 large red onions, sliced

1 sprig of thyme

For the sandwich

1 tablespoon butter

2 tablespoons olive oil

4 x 200g (7oz) fillet steaks

2 ciabatta loaves

2 heads of baby little gem, stems removed

juice of ½ lemon

2 large beef tomatoes, thickly sliced

Method

- To prepare the mustard, put all the dry ingredients in a processor or blender and blend until the seeds are roughly crushed.
- With the motor still running, gradually pour in the vinegar and blend until well mixed, then add the stout and blend briefly.
- Leave the mustard to stand for 1 hour to thicken, then transfer to warm, dry, sterilized jars. Cover the surface of each with a disc of waxed paper, waxed side down, and leave until cold. Top the cold jars with airtight lids, label and store in a cool, dark place. The mustard should keep for 3–6 months
- Preheat the oven to 180°C/350°F/Gas mark 4.
- To prepare the onions, heat a pan until hot, then add the butter, 1 tablespoon of the olive oil, onions and thyme. Reduce the heat and cook slowly for 12–15 minutes until tender and caramelized
- Meanwhile, prepare the steaks. Heat another frying pan until hot and add the butter and olive oil.
- Season the steaks, add to the pan and cook for 2–4 minutes, or until they are cooked to your liking. Remove from the pan and leave to rest for a few minutes.
- Place the ciabatta in the oven for 5 minutes to warm through.
- Dress the little gem leaves with the lemon juice and the remaining tablespoon of olive oil.
- To serve, cut the ciabatta loaves in half, then split them lengthways and place on a board.
- Cut the fillet steaks on an angle into 1cm thick slices.
- Spread some of the mustard onto the bottom slice of each sandwich and top with some of the dressed little gem leaves.
- Place the steak slices on top of the little gem leaves and top with the caramelized red onions.
- Place the lids on top of the sandwiches and serve.

Wine expert Jancis Robinson's choice
Calvet-Thunevin Cuvee Constance

Richard E Grant

Food heaven: prawns

Richard was brought up in Swaziland and loved the huge African prawns he ate growing up.

'We would sometimes go on day trips to Mozambique, where we would feast on prawns. I love them still. We had a typically British colonial diet and I remember living off tinned foods a lot of the time, and although Swazi fruit was amazing, it was only available at certain times of the year.'

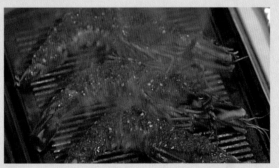

piri-piri prawns and harissa couscous

Serves 4

Ingredients

For the piri-piri prawns

2 red chillies, roughly chopped

1 dried chilli, roughly chopped

juice of ½ lemon

3 cloves garlic

1 tablespoon sweet smoked paprika

4 tablespoons olive oil

1 tablespoon red wine vinegar

1 tablespoon sea salt

½ teaspoon freshly ground black
  pepper

12 very large African prawns, shelled
  but tails retained

For the couscous

200g (7oz) wholegrain couscous

400ml (14fl oz) boiling water

1 teaspoon rose harissa

1 tablespoon pomegranate molasses

1 teaspoon baharat spice mix

juice of ½ lemon

1 red onion, finely sliced

1 pomegranate

1 small bunch of coriander, roughly
  chopped

extra lemon juice, to serve

Method

- To prepare the prawns, place all the ingredients except the prawns in a small blender and process until smooth.
- Place the prawns on a plate, pour the piri-piri sauce over and combine well, making sure the prawns are fully coated. Set aside in the fridge to marinate for 1 hour.
- Meanwhile, place the couscous in a bowl, pour over the boiling water and stir to combine.
- Add the harissa, molasses, baharat spices and lemon juice and stir once more.
- Cover with cling film and set aside for 3–4 minutes, or until all the liquid has been absorbed into the couscous. Remove the cling film and fluff up with a fork.
- Add the red onion, pomegranate seeds and coriander and mix well.
- Heat a griddle pan until hot.
- Place the prawns on the griddle and cook for 2–3 minutes on each side, depending on the size.
- To serve, place some prawns on each plate with a pile of couscous alongside. Drizzle with the piri-piri marinade and a squeeze of lemon juice.

Wine expert Olly Smith's choice

Otra Vida Viognier

Eddie Jordan

Food heaven: crab

'I relish my food. I like natural, simple, local food. I have a boat moored off Corsica. The Captain is a submarine officer and a trained diver so he goes down and catches sea urchins, oysters and other delicious treats and I bung them onto the barbeque – wonderful! I love all shellfish but crab is my absolute favourite.'

crab patties with mizuna salad and chilli dressing

Serves 4

Ingredients

For the crab patties

600g (1lb 5oz) fresh white crab meat

400g (14oz) floury potatoes, cooked, mashed and cooled

1 x 1cm piece of ginger, finely grated

juice of 1 lime

1 small bunch of coriander, roughly chopped

1 tablespoon olive oil

salt

black pepper

For the salad

2 red chillies, finely diced

75g (3oz) caster sugar

75ml (3fl oz) white wine vinegar

75ml (3fl oz) water

75g (3oz) mizuna leaves

50g (2oz) sweetcorn

4 spring onions, finely sliced

50g (2oz) fresh coconut, sliced and toasted in a dry frying pan until golden

Method

- Place the crab, potato, ginger and lime juice in a bowl and mix thoroughly, then add the coriander and season with salt and black pepper.
- Take golf ball-sized pieces of the crab mix and form into flat patties.
- Heat a frying pan until hot and add the olive oil. Fry the patties on both sides until golden-brown and heated through.
- To prepare the salad, place the chillies, sugar, vinegar and water in a saucepan and bring to the boil, then reduce the heat and simmer for 5 minutes to make the dressing.
- Place the mizuna leaves, sweetcorn, spring onions and coconut in a bowl and toss to combine. Add a little dressing and toss once more.
- To serve, place a pile of the dressed salad on each plate and top with a couple of crab patties.

Wine expert Olly Smith's choice
Casablanca Chardonnay

John Barrowman

Food heaven: meringue

John has a very sweet tooth and especially loves meringue, toffee and vanilla.

His earliest food memories are of meat pies in Glasgow. 'Growing up, my mother would always take me to a local bakery for pie. I would get the traditional Scottish pie made with mutton and would have it with beans. I am very nostalgic about pies and can cook a mean pie myself these days!'

toffee baked Alaska with toffee sauce

Serves 8

Ingredients

For the baked Alaska

50ml (2fl oz) water

225g (8oz) white caster sugar

4 egg whites

75g (3oz) hazelnuts, finely chopped

1 small chocolate sponge

500g (1lb 2oz) vanilla ice cream

500g (1lb 2oz) toffee ice cream

For the toffee sauce

500ml (18fl oz) double cream

175g (6oz) demerara sugar

175g (6oz) butter

1 tablespoon golden syrup

1 tablespoon black treacle

Method

- For the baked Alaska, place the water and sugar in a saucepan and bring to the boil. Skim the surface and wipe the sides of the pan with a pastry brush to remove any crystals, then increase the heat so that the syrup boils rapidly.
- Insert a sugar thermometer. When the sugar reaches 110°C/225°F, beat the egg whites with an electric mixer until stiff peaks are formed.
- When the sugar reaches 130°C/250°F, remove from the heat.
- Turn the electric mixer onto the lowest setting, then pour the sugar syrup into the egg whites in a thin, steady stream until all the syrup is incorporated.
- Continue to beat at a slow speed until the mixture is almost cold. This could take up to 15 minutes.
- Fold the hazelnuts into the meringue mixture, then spoon it into a piping bag fitted with a plain nozzle.
- Place the sponge on the serving plate and top with alternate scoops of vanilla and toffee ice cream.
- Pipe the meringue around the ice cream, covering completely from top to bottom. Glaze the meringue with a blow torch or bake briefly in a very hot oven.
- For the toffee sauce, put the cream in a saucepan and heat gently.
- Add the sugar and butter and whisk until melted, then whisk in the syrup and treacle.
- To serve, place a wedge of baked Alaska on each plate and drizzle the sauce over the top.

Wine expert Peter Richards's choice

Concha y Toro Late Harvest Sauvignon Blanc

Sally Gunnell

Food heaven: chicken

'Throughout my life, and particularly when I was an athlete, I've relied fairly heavily on chicken as part of my diet. I love chicken thighs particularly.

As an athlete, I always had to be careful with what I ate.

I like Chinese food, but it is so unhealthy. Whenever I wanted to treat myself, we would have Thai food, as it is quite healthy and fresh, yet delicious.'

Thai green chicken curry with potatoes, pea aubergines and lemon grass jasmine rice

Serves 2

Ingredients

For the curry

1 tablespoon vegetable oil

2 banana shallots, finely sliced

2 tablespoons Thai green curry paste

400ml (14fl oz) coconut milk

1 teaspoon fish sauce

4 chicken thighs, boneless and
  skinless

250g (9oz) new potatoes, peeled
  and halved

125g (4½oz) pea aubergines

juice of 1 lime

salt

black pepper

For the rice

250g (9oz) Thai jasmine rice

1 lemon grass stem, bashed

500ml (18fl oz) cold water

1 small bunch of coriander, leaves
  picked

Method

- To prepare the curry, heat a high-sided frying pan until hot, then add the vegetable oil and shallots.
- Stir fry for 1 minute, then add the Thai green curry paste and stir fry for a further minute.
- Add the coconut milk and bring to the boil.
- Add the fish sauce, chicken thighs, potatoes and aubergines and return to a simmer, then cover with a lid and simmer on a low heat for 15–20 minutes until the chicken is cooked through and the potatoes are tender.
- Add the lime juice and season with salt and black pepper.
- Meanwhile, place the rice and lemon grass in a small saucepan with the water, cover with a lid and place on the heat.
- Bring to the boil, then reduce the heat and simmer gently for 12–15 minutes until tender and all the water is absorbed. Remove the lemon grass.
- To serve, pile some rice on each plate, top with some curry and sprinkle over the coriander leaves.

Wine expert Olly Smith's choice

Martin Codax Albariño

Jackie Collins

Food heaven: onions

'I love finely chopped white onions that have been fried in butter.'
Jackie loves mashed potato 'with butter, milk, sour cream and
chopped onions'. In fact, she loves chopped onion, full stop.
'Michael Caine taught me how to cook Yorkshire pudding. He loves
to cook and every Sunday I would go to theirs for lunch.'

French onion soup with cheese croûte, red onion compote and fried shallots

Serves 4–6

Ingredients

For the soup

25g (1oz) butter

2 tablespoons olive oil

1kg (2lb 2oz) white onions, finely
   sliced

3 cloves garlic, finely chopped

2 sprigs of thyme, leaves picked

50ml (2fl oz) dry sherry

75ml (3fl oz) brandy

250ml (9fl oz) white wine

1 teaspoon soft brown sugar

1 litre (1 pint 15fl oz) fresh beef stock

1 tablespoon balsamic vinegar

1 small French baguette, sliced
   diagonally

110g (4oz) Gruyère cheese, grated

salt

black pepper

For the red onion compote

1 tablespoon olive oil

1 red onion, finely sliced

½ teaspoon soft brown sugar

1 tablespoon balsamic vinegar

juice of ½ lemon

salt

black pepper

For the shallot rings

vegetable oil, for deep-frying

2 shallots, sliced into rings

2 tablespoons plain flour

Method

· To prepare the soup, heat a wide, deep-sided frying pan until hot, then add the butter, olive oil, onions, garlic and thyme.

· Fry for 20–25 minutes over a medium-low heat until softened and golden-brown.

· Add the sherry, two-thirds of the brandy and the wine and flambé.

· When the flames have died down, add the sugar and beef stock, bring to the boil and simmer for 10 minutes.

· Season with salt and black pepper, then add the balsamic vinegar and remaining brandy.

· Preheat the grill to high.

· Grill the bread on one side, then turn, cover with Gruyère and grill until golden and bubbling.

· Meanwhile, prepare the compote. Heat a frying pan until hot, then add the olive oil and red onion.

· Fry for 5–8 minutes until just softened but not too browned.

· Add the sugar, vinegar and lemon juice and season with salt and black pepper.

· To prepare the shallot rings, heat vegetable oil in a deep-fat fryer to 190°C/375°F.

· Season the flour with salt and black pepper and toss the shallot rings in the seasoned flour.

· Drop into the fryer and fry for 1–2 minutes until golden, then remove and drain on kitchen paper.

· To serve, ladle some soup into each serving bowl and top with a cheesy croûte. Top each croûte with a spoonful of compote and a few onion rings.

Wine expert Susy Atkins's choice
Les Pierblancs Sauvignon Blanc

hell

Tom Parker-Bowles

Food hell: goats' cheese

Tom was in no doubt about his food hell.

'It has to be goats' cheese. I've never licked the floor of a pigsty, but if
I did lick one, I imagine the taste would be the same as goats' cheese.
It has sort of a chalky, slightly urine-type flavour. Everyone else loves it,
but I just can't eat the stuff.'

chicken breast stuffed and topped with goats' cheese with roasted vegetables and potatoes

Serves 2

Ingredients

2 boneless, skinless chicken breasts

150g soft goats' cheese, sliced

3 tablespoons olive oil

1 crotin goats' cheese, sliced

1 pepper, quartered

1 courgette, cut lengthways into 5mm thick strips

1 aubergine, cut into 5mm thick rounds

200g (7oz) cooked baby new potatoes, cut in half

salt

black pepper

Method

- Preheat the oven to 200°C/400°F/Gas Mark 6.
- Use a sharp knife to cut a pocket in the side of each chicken breast and carefully ease them open.
- Press the slices of soft goats' cheese into the pockets, then season the breasts with salt and black pepper.
- Heat a frying pan until hot, then add 1 tablespoon of the olive oil. Add the chicken breasts, presentation side down, and fry until golden-brown, then turn them over and cook for a further 2 minutes.
- Transfer the pan to the oven for 15 minutes.
- Remove, top with the crotin goats' cheese and return to the oven for a further 5 minutes until the cheese has melted.
- Meanwhile, heat a griddle pan until really hot.
- Toss the pepper, courgette and aubergine with the remaining olive oil, season, then place on the griddle pan and cook for 5 minutes until tender, turning once.
- To serve, place a chicken breast on each plate with a pile of charred vegetables and some cooked potatoes alongside.

Wine expert Olly Smith's choice
Unité Chardonnay Cave de Lugny

Wendy Richards

Food hell: salmon

'I don't like salmon in any form. I always get given smoked salmon as a starter wherever I go – particularly charity events and I have gotten sick of it. I also particularly dislike fresh salmon which I find far too rich.

My style of cooking is definitely traditional English food. I like to cook steak pies, Sunday roasts and I make an excellent chilli con carne.'

poached salmon with griddled asparagus, lemon mayonnaise and salad

Serves 6–8

Ingredients

For the salmon

1 x 2½kg (5lb 6oz) whole salmon, scaled and gutted

1 onion, quartered

2 bay leaves

4 tablespoons white wine vinegar

1 lemon, quartered

salt

black pepper

For the mayonnaise

2 egg yolks

1 teaspoon white vinegar

½ teaspoon powdered mustard

1 teaspoon salt

1 lemon, juiced

275ml (10fl oz) rapeseed oil

For the salad

24 asparagus spears

3 tablespoons olive oil

6 thick slices white bread, cut into 1cm cubes

2 spears of rosemary

½ teaspoon Dijon mustard

1 tablespoon white wine vinegar

3 tablespoons extra virgin olive oil

2 heads of baby little gem lettuce, leaves separated

salt

black pepper

Method

- To prepare the salmon, place it either in a fish kettle or a large roasting tin and pour over enough cold water to cover the fish.
- Add the onion, bay leaves, vinegar, lemon, a good pinch of salt and a few twists of black pepper.
- Cover with a lid or tin foil and bring to the boil. As soon as it boils, turn off the heat and leave the fish to stand in the water until it has cooled to room temperature.
- Carefully remove the salmon from its cooking juices, transfer to a chopping board and scrape off the skin and discard. Put the salmon on a large, flat serving dish.
- To prepare the mayonnaise, place the egg yolks, vinegar, mustard, salt and lemon juice in a food processor.
- Blend to combine, then, with the motor still running, gradually add the rapeseed oil until all the oil has been added and the mayonnaise has thickened. Season with black pepper and a little more salt if necessary.
- To prepare the salad, preheat a griddle pan until hot.
- Toss the asparagus spears with 1 tablespoon of the olive oil and season with salt and black pepper.
- Place on the griddle and cook for 2–3 minutes until charred and just tender, then remove and set aside.
- Heat a frying pan until hot and add the remaining olive oil, the bread cubes and the rosemary.
- Fry for 2–3 minutes until the bread is golden and crispy, then drain onto kitchen paper.
- Place the mustard in a bowl along with the vinegar and whisk in the extra virgin olive oil. Season with salt and black pepper and toss with the little gem leaves. Add the croutons and toss once more.
- To serve, place some asparagus spears on each plate with a spoonful of dressed salad. Carefully lift some cooked salmon off the bone and onto each plate. Serve with a dollop of lemon mayonnaise alongside.

Wine expert Peter Richards's choice

Nobilo Marlborough Sauvignon Blanc

Chris Evans

Food hell: puddings

'My food hell is puddings because I do not see the point of them –
everyone is stuffed by the pudding stage of a meal. They are irrelevant
and useless and I don't believe that anyone enjoys them, including
James Martin. For me, it is all about the starter and the main course.
I love a bit of cheese and port as well, so where is the need for a
pudding?'

Christmas pudding and ice cream filo parcels with brandy sauce

Serves 6

Ingredients

For the parcels

500g (18oz) vanilla ice cream

450g (1lb) Christmas pudding

12 sheets ready-made filo pastry

50g (2oz) butter, melted

3 tablespoons icing sugar

For the brandy sauce

200ml (7fl oz) double cream

600ml (1 pint) full-fat milk

25g (1oz) cornflour, mixed with 4
   tablespoons cold water

50g (2oz) granulated sugar

50g (2oz) unsalted butter

3–4 tablespoons brandy

Method

- Preheat the oven to 240°C/475°F/Gas Mark 9.
- Scoop the ice cream into 6 balls, place them on a baking sheet and put in the freezer until ready to use.
- Scoop out a handful of Christmas pudding and lay between 2 pieces of cling film. Using a rolling pin, flatten the pudding to about 1cm thick. Repeat to create 6 pudding sheets.
- Remove the top sheet of cling film from one pudding sheet and place an ice cream scoop in the centre. Draw the pudding around the ice cream to cover totally. Place in the freezer, then repeat with the remaining pudding sheets.
- Lay 1 sheet of filo pastry on a board and brush with melted butter. Place one pudding ball in the centre and draw the filo pastry up around the pudding ball to cover totally, making sure the pastry is well sealed. Repeat this process to encase it in another layer of filo, then return to the freezer and repeat until all the pudding balls are covered.
- Place the pudding parcels on a baking sheet, then dust with the icing sugar and place in the oven for 8–10 minutes.
- To make the brandy sauce, place the cream and milk in a saucepan and bring to the boil.
- Stir in the cornflour solution and return to the boil, stirring constantly to thicken.
- Remove from the heat and stir in the sugar and butter, continuing to stir until totally dissolved, then add the brandy and stir again.
- To serve, place a pudding parcel in each bowl and pour over some of the hot brandy sauce.

Wine expert Susie Barrie's choice
Pedro Ximenez Viejo Napoleon, Hidalgo

Al Murray

Food hell: rice

'What is the point of rice? Tell me! When I see a dollop of rice on a plate with a curry, I think, "What a let-down". Give me spuds any day of the week. Rice is just bland and boring. I cannot stand the stuff. I love cooking. My tip is an extra quid or two spent on good quality ingredients will make all the difference, consequently the food can be simpler and more delicious.'

baked rice pudding with raspberry sauce

Serves 6

Ingredients

For the rice pudding

110g (4oz) Thai jasmine rice

450ml (16fl oz) full-fat milk
   (preferably organic)

450ml (16fl oz) double cream

1 vanilla pod, split

75g (3oz) caster sugar

25g (1oz) butter, plus extra for
   greasing

freshly grated nutmeg

6 tablespoons icing sugar

For the raspberry sauce

250g (9oz) raspberries

2 tablespoons icing sugar

50ml (2fl oz) water

Method

· Preheat the oven to 180°C/350°F/Gas Mark 4.

· Lightly grease a pudding basin or ovenproof dish (about 1 litre/
  1¾ pints in size).

· Rinse the rice under cold water and drain.

· Place the milk and cream in a saucepan with the vanilla pod and bring
  to the boil.

· Add the rice and caster sugar and stir well.

· Pour into the pudding basin or dish, grate a little nutmeg over the top
  and dot with knobs of the butter.

· Place in the oven and bake for about 15 minutes, then lower the
  temperature to 150°C/300°F/Gas Mark 2.

· Bake for a further 1½ hours until golden-brown on top and creamy
  underneath.

· Dust with the icing sugar and place under the grill to caramelize,
  or use a blowtorch.

· Meanwhile, prepare the raspberry sauce. Place all the ingredients in
  a blender and purée well until smooth.

· Pass through a fine sieve, pushing it through with a spatula or spoon.

· To serve, spoon some of the sauce into each bowl and top with a
  large spoonful of rice pudding.

Wine expert Tim Atkin's choice

Domaine Cady Les Chavagnes, Coteaux du Layon

Matt Baker

Food hell: bread

'I find bread too stuffing and stodgy. I would quite happily eat the filling of a sandwich and not the bread.

We went on an expedition for Blue Peter to Iceland. It is a bit of a tradition for the males to challenge one another in eating grotesque things. Rotten shark is one of these. It was definitely the worst meal I have ever eaten in my life. My eyes were watering with the smell and taste.'

white chocolate and whisky bread and butter pudding

Serves 4

Ingredients

350ml (12fl oz) milk

350ml (12fl oz) double cream

1 vanilla pod, split

2 whole eggs

4 egg yolks

150g (5oz) caster sugar

8–10 slices white bread, cut into quarters

25g (1oz) sultanas

110g (4oz) butter, melted

150g (6oz) white chocolate, roughly chopped

60ml (2½fl oz) whisky

2 tablespoons icing sugar, to dust

Method

· Preheat the oven to 180C/Gas 4.

· Place the milk, cream and vanilla pod into a saucepan and bring to the boil.

· Place the eggs, egg yolks and sugar into a bowl and whisk to combine.

· when the cream mixture has boiled, remove from the heat and whisk the egg mixture into it.

· Add the white chocolate and whisk until smooth.

· Meanwhile, butter an ovenproof dish and place the bread into it, overlapping the slices.

· Add the whisky and pour over the bread, then scatter over the sultanas.

· Place in the oven for 20–25 minutes until golden and just set.

· Remove from the oven and dust with icing sugar.

· Place under the grill to caramelize or use a blowtorch.

· Serve with a spoonful of ice cream.

Wine expert Olly Smith's choice

La Copita Sweet Oloroso

Robert Bathurst

Food hell: Mexican food

'Three days into our honeymoon in Central America I had a meal of chicken tacos. I got salmonella, and six weeks later I returned home two stone lighter. My new wife had to do a lot of sightseeing on her own in the interim! Now just the thought of a Mexican meal turns my stomach and I have not been able to revisit tortillas or refried beans since.'

chicken and cheese quesadilla, refried bean chimichanga and sweetcorn chilli salsa

Serves 4

Ingredients

For the quesadilla

8 ready-made flour tortillas

250g (9oz) mature cheddar, grated

300g (11oz) cooked chicken breast,
thickly sliced

½ red onion, finely sliced

60g (2½oz) jalapeno chillies, roughly
chopped

1 small bunch of coriander

4 tablespoons sour cream

2 tablespoons olive oil

For the chimichanga

1 x 435g (15oz) tin refried beans

½ red chilli, finely diced

juice of 1 lime

110g (4oz) tinned black-eyed beans,
rinsed and drained

2 spring onions, roughly chopped

3 tablespoons roughly chopped
coriander

4 ready-made flour tortillas

1 egg, beaten

vegetable oil, for deep-fat frying

For the salsa

150g (5oz) sweetcorn

20g (¾oz) jalapeno chillies, roughly
chopped

1 green chilli, finely chopped

juice of 1 lime

2 tablespoons roughly chopped mint
leaves

2 tablespoons roughly chopped
coriander leaves

Method

- To prepare the quesadillas, place 4 of the tortillas on a board and cover each with the grated cheese.
- Top with the chicken, red onion, jalapeno chillies and coriander.
- Spread the sour cream on the remaining 4 tortillas and place them, cream side down, on top of the filled tortillas.
- Heat a frying pan until medium hot and add the olive oil.
- Carefully place one quesadilla in the frying pan and cook over a medium heat for 3–4 minutes until it is golden and crispy and the cheese has melted. Flip over and cook on the other side for a further 2 minutes. Repeat with the remaining quesadillas.
- To prepare the chimichangas, heat a deep-fat fryer to 190°C/375°F/Gas Mark 5.
- Place the refried beans, chilli, lime juice, black-eyed beans, spring onions and coriander in a bowl and mix well.
- Spoon the mixture into the centre of each of the 4 tortillas.
- Fold each end of each tortilla inwards, then roll them up into cigar shapes. Brush the final edge of each tortilla with the beaten egg, to seal the parcels.
- Place in the deep-fat fryer and cook for 3–4 minutes until golden and heated through, then drain onto kitchen paper.
- To prepare the salsa, place all the ingredients in a food processor and pulse to combine, then season to taste.
- To serve, cut each quesadilla into quarters and each chimichanga in half and arrange around each plate. Place a small bowl of salsa in the middle of each plate.

Wine expert Susie Barrie's choice

Finca Flichman Misterio Malbec, Argentina

Samantha Janus

Food hell: walnuts

'For me, it is all about strange combinations. Pineapple on pizza makes me feel funny, but Waldorf salad is the worst. It is the walnuts combined with fruit and celery that doesn't work for me. I love most foods but I am not keen generally on nuts and walnuts have definitely got to be up there around the top of my dislikes list. They are definitely my idea of food hell!'

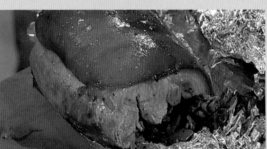

walnut and apple stuffed rolled loin of pork with roasted honey and walnut parsnips

Serves 6

Ingredients

For the pork

150g (5oz) walnuts, roughly chopped

2 green apples, diced

2 sprigs of thyme, roughly chopped

200g (7oz) butter, softened, plus
   extra for greasing

1kg (2lb 2oz) boneless loin of pork

1–2 tablespoons vegetable oil

salt

black pepper

For the parsnips

6 parsnips, peeled and quartered

3 tablespoons olive oil

4 tablespoons honey

2 sprigs of thyme

100g (3½oz) walnut halves

ready-made gravy, to serve

salt

black pepper

Method

- Preheat the oven to 200°C/400°F/Gas Mark 6.
- Place the walnuts, apples, thyme and two-thirds of the butter in a bowl and mix to combine to a chunky paste, then season with salt and black pepper.
- Lay the pork flesh side up on a chopping board, with the belly flap facing away from you. With a sharp knife, make an incision in the meat halfway down, running parallel to the board, cutting almost all the way through. Open the loin up and season with salt and pepper, then stuff the loin with the butter mixture, spreading it to the edges of the meat.
- Grease a piece of foil large enough to wrap the loin in and place the loin on top. Roll it in the foil to form a sausage shape, twist the ends of the foil so the parcel is very tight and tie with some string.
- Heat a large roasting tin on the hob until hot and add the vegetable oil.
- Put the foil parcel in the tin and cook, turning every 2 minutes until all parts of the parcel have had contact with the heat.
- Put into the oven and roast for 1–1½ hours.
- Meanwhile, prepare the parsnips. Place them in a roasting tin, drizzle over the olive oil and honey and toss to combine.
- Season with salt and black pepper and add the thyme sprigs.
- Place in the oven and roast for 30–35 minutes until tender and golden.
- Add the walnuts and return to the oven for 5 minutes.
- To serve, unwrap the loin parcel and cut into thick slices. Put a slice on each plate with a heap of parsnips alongside and drizzle with gravy.

Wine expert Susy Atkins's choice
Cono Sur Pinot Noir

Jenny Agutter

Food hell: butter beans

'I have memories of school food and very particularly butter beans, which always came swimming in water. Taste, for me, has a lot to do with texture, and there's something awfully floury about butter beans. I just don't like them.'

Jenny's an accomplished cook and grows a lot of her own ingredients. 'We have a house in Cornwall with a vegetable garden with broad beans, potatoes, green runner beans, courgettes amongst other things. But no butter beans!'

duck confit with butter bean mash, tomato and butter bean compote and red wine sauce

Serves 4

Ingredients

For the duck confit

4 duck legs

1 tablespoon table salt per kg of
   duck leg

2–3 sprigs of fresh thyme, leaves
   picked

300g (11oz) duck fat

4 tablespoons clear honey

6 tablespoons extra virgin olive oil

For the butter bean mash

600g (1lb 5oz) King Edward potatoes,
   peeled and cut into chunks

1 x 400g (14oz) tin butter beans,
   rinsed and drained

2 tablespoons extra virgin olive oil

75ml (3fl oz) milk

salt

white pepper

**For the butter bean and tomato
compote and red wine sauce**

1 tablespoon olive oil

1 onion, chopped

2 cloves garlic, chopped

2 sprigs of thyme

2 x 400g (14oz) tin chopped tomatoes

110ml (4fl oz) white wine

1 x 400g (14oz) tin butter beans,
   rinsed and drained

2 tablespoons roughly chopped
   flat-leaf parsley

25g (1oz) butter

½ red onion, thickly sliced

750ml (1 pint 6fl oz) fresh beef stock

250ml (9fl oz) red wine

salt

black pepper

Method

- To prepare the duck confit, weigh the duck legs, place them on a baking tray and sprinkle with a tablespoon of salt per kilo and the thyme. Wrap with cling film and place in the fridge overnight.
- Heat a heavy pan until warm and add the duck legs. Add the duck fat to completely cover the legs.
- Bring the fat to a gentle simmer and cook slowly for about 2 to 2½ hours until very tender, then remove the legs from the fat and place on a roasting tray, draining off the excess fat.
- Preheat the oven to 180°C/350°F/Gas Mark 4.
- Whisk the honey and oil together and smear over the duck legs.
- Roast the legs in the oven for about 20 minutes, basting them with more of the honey glaze a couple of times.
- To prepare the mash, place the potatoes and butter beans in a saucepan of water to cover and bring to the boil.
- Reduce the heat and simmer for 15 minutes, then drain and place the potatoes and beans in a large bowl. Add the olive oil and milk and mash to a purée. Season with salt and white pepper.
- To prepare the compote, heat a deep-sided frying pan until hot, add the olive oil, onion and garlic and sauté for 3 minutes.
- Add the thyme, tomatoes and white wine and bring to the boil, then reduce the heat and simmer for 15–20 minutes until thickened.
- Add the beans and simmer for a further 15 minutes, season with salt and black pepper and stir in the chopped parsley.
- To prepare the sauce, heat a frying pan until hot and add half the butter and all the onion. Sauté the onion until well browned, then add the stock and red wine. Simmer the sauce until it has reduced by half and slightly thickened, then pass through a sieve.
- Whisk in the remaining butter and season with salt and black pepper.
- Place a spoonful of the bean mash on each plate and top with a duck leg and serve with the compote and sauce spooned around.

Wine expert Olly Smith's choice
Cono Sur Reserva Pinot Noir

Lisa Snowdon

Food hell: Stilton

'My food hell would be Stilton. It looks and smells awful to me and is so overpowering. I remember that my dad always had Stilton in the fridge at Christmas, and it would turn my stomach and stink the whole fridge out. It is such a strong flavour and dominates everything it is prepared with. I prefer flavours to complement one another.'

Parma ham wrapped Stilton, chicken and green bean loaf

Serves 4–6

Ingredients

For the loaf

2 chicken breasts, boneless
  and skinless
1 tablespoon olive oil
225g (8oz) green beans, topped
  and tailed
12 slices Parma ham
500g (1lb 2oz) Stilton, thickly sliced
salt
black pepper

For the salad

150g (5oz) green beans, trimmed
150g (5oz) broad beans, podded
1 bunch of rocket
75g (3oz) walnuts, roughly chopped
1 teaspoon Dijon mustard
2 tablespoons white wine vinegar
6 tablespoons extra virgin olive oil
110g (4oz) Stilton
salt
black pepper

Method

- Preheat the oven to 190C/375F/Gas Mark 5.
- To prepare the loaf, season the chicken breasts with salt and black pepper and rub with the olive oil.
- Place the breasts in a roasting tin and place in the oven for 20 minutes, or until cooked through. Remove from the oven and allow to cool slightly, then slice them thickly and set to one side.
- Meanwhile, bring a small pan of lightly salted water to the boil and drop in the green beans.
- Cook for 5–6 minutes until tender, then drain and refresh in iced water and drain once more.
- Line a small loaf tin with cling film. Drape the Parma ham into the loaf tin, covering the bottom and sides, leaving a little excess hanging over the top of the tin to pull over the top.
- Place half the chicken slices in the bottom of the tin and top with a layer of Stilton. Top with half the green beans, laying them lengthways down the length of the tin. Repeat with another layer of chicken, Stilton and beans.
- Using the cling film, pull the Parma ham over the top of the last layer of beans to enclose totally.
- Place a couple of heavy tins on top to compress the loaf and place in the fridge for 1 hour to set.
- Meanwhile, prepare the salad. Bring a small pan of lightly salted water to the boil and drop in the green beans.
- Cook for 5–6 minutes until tender, then drain and refresh in iced water and drain once more.
- Place in a bowl along with the broad beans, rocket and walnuts.
- In a small bowl, whisk the mustard, vinegar and olive oil together, then crumble in the Stilton cheese and season with salt and black pepper.
- Pour the dressing over the salad and toss together.
- Place 2 thick slices of loaf on each plate along with a spoonful of the dressed salad.

Wine expert Susie Barrie's choice
Fetzer Zinfandel/Shiraz

Jessica Hynes

Food hell: sardines

'I hate sardines! They are too bony and it makes them difficult to cook and eat. I always find they are too small to fillet, yet unless they're tinned you can't eat them whole. I find them very irritating to deal with.' Jessica sent temperatures soaring when she helped cook her food hell. Her sardines burst into flames under the grill, but luckily James was close at hand to save the day.

grilled sardines with sauce vierge, pan-fried Jersey royals and salad

Serves 4

Ingredients

For the sardines

12 sardines, cleaned and gutted

For the potatoes

1 tablespoon olive oil

200g (8oz) Jersey royal potatoes, scrubbed and par-boiled

For the sauce vierge

100ml (3½fl oz) extra virgin olive oil

juice of 1 lemon

2 tomatoes, skinned, seeded and diced

1 shallot, finely diced

1 small clove garlic, finely diced

2 tablespoons roughly chopped tarragon

2 tablespoons roughly chopped basil

2 tablespoons roughly chopped dill

salt

black pepper

For the salad

110g (4oz) mixed salad leaves

3 tablespoons extra virgin olive oil

1 tablespoon balsamic vinegar

Method

- Preheat the grill to high.
- Remove the head from the sardines, then cut open along the belly from the head end to the tail and open out, flesh side down. Press down along the body with the heel of your hand, then turn over and lift out the bones.
- Place on a grill tray and season with salt and black pepper, then grill for 3–4 minutes until cooked through.
- To prepare the potatoes, heat a frying pan until hot and add the olive oil and potatoes. Fry for 3–4 minutes until golden and crispy, then season with salt and black pepper.
- To prepare the sauce vierge, place the extra virgin olive oil in a saucepan and whisk in the lemon juice.
- Add the tomatoes, shallot and garlic and place on the heat to just warm through, then add the herbs and season with salt and black pepper.
- Toss the salad leaves with the extra virgin olive oil and balsamic vinegar.
- To serve, divide the potatoes among 4 plates and top each pile with 3 sardines. Spoon over the warm sauce vierge and place some dressed salad leaves alongside.

Wine expert Tim Atkin's choice

La Différence Viognier/Muscat

Griff Rhys Jones

Food hell: stew

Griff's food hell is based on his bad recollections of school food. 'It dates back to when I was a little boy. In those days we just used to eat stews at school and you never knew quite what was in them. Bits of fat and gristly stuff would be floating in them.'

beef stew and dumplings

Serves 4

Ingredients

For the beef stew

2 tablespoons olive oil

25g (1oz) butter

750g (1lb 11oz) stewing beef steak, diced

2 tablespoons plain flour

2 cloves garlic, crushed

175g (6oz) baby onions, peeled

150g (5oz) celery, cut into large chunks

150g (5oz) carrots, cut into large chunks

2 leeks, roughly chopped

200g (7oz) swede, cut into large chunks

150ml (5fl oz) red wine

500ml (18fl oz) beef stock

2 bay leaves

3 tablespoons fresh thyme leaves

3 tablespoons chopped flat-leaf parsley

Worcestershire sauce, to taste

1 tablespoon balsamic vinegar

salt

black pepper, freshly ground

For dumplings

125g (4½oz) plain flour

1 teaspoon baking powder

1 pinch of salt

60g (2½oz) suet

To serve

mashed potato

1 tablespoon roughly chopped flat-leaf parsley

Method

- Preheat the oven to 180°C/350°F/Gas Mark 4.
- To prepare the beef stew, heat an ovenproof casserole dish until hot, then add the oil, butter and beef and fry until browned.
- Add the flour and continue to cook for 2–3 minutes.
- Add the garlic and all the vegetables and cook for 1–2 minutes.
- Stir in the wine, stock and herbs, then add the Worcestershire sauce and balsamic vinegar. Season with salt and freshly ground black pepper.
- Cover with a lid, transfer to the oven and cook for about 2 hours until the meat is tender.
- Meanwhile, prepare the dumplings. Sieve the flour, baking powder and salt into a bowl.
- Add the suet and enough water to form a thick dough. Flour your hands and form small dough balls.
- Remove the lid from the stew, place the balls on the top of the stew and cover.
- Return to the oven and cook for a further 20 minutes until the dumplings have swollen and are tender.
- To serve, place a spoonful of mash on each plate, place a portion of stew alongside, topped with a few dumplings, and sprinkle the chopped parsley over.

Wine expert Olly Smith's choice
Wakefield Shiraz

Patsy Palmer

Food hell: smoked salmon

'I like fresh salmon, but there is something about smoked salmon that I really can't stand. Maybe it is the texture, as I find it quite slimy, and I really don't like the smell.

My husband and his family are so passionate about cooking and food in general. When I got married my mother-in-law taught me how to cook. They basically taught me to make everything from scratch and to cook with fresh ingredients.'

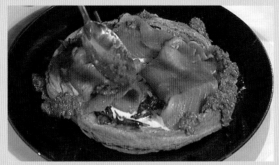

smoked salmon and spinach tart with watercress pesto and salad

Serves 4

Ingredients

For the tart

500g (1lb 2oz) all-butter puff pastry
500g (1lb 2oz) baby leaf spinach
1 pinch of grated nutmeg
250g (9oz) crème fraîche
1 egg
325g (11½oz) smoked salmon, sliced
salt
black pepper

For the pesto

110g (4oz) watercress
20g (¾oz) walnuts
75ml (3fl oz) extra virgin olive oil
salt
black pepper

For the salad

150g (5oz) watercress
2 tablespoons walnut oil
2 teaspoons red wine vinegar

Method

· Preheat the oven to 200°C/400°F/Gas Mark 6.
· To prepare the tart, roll out the pastry to 5mm thick and stamp out four 15cm circles. Place on a baking sheet and pierce several times with a fork.
· Place in the oven and bake for 10 minutes until golden and risen.
· Meanwhile, heat a frying pan until hot, add the spinach and cook until wilted. Season with salt, black pepper and a pinch of nutmeg, then remove from the pan and squeeze out any excess water.
· Whisk the crème fraîche and egg together and season with salt and black pepper.
· Divide the spinach among the tarts, then spoon some of the crème fraîche over the top of the spinach and top with slices of smoked salmon.
· Return to the oven for 5 minutes until the salmon has cooked through.
· To prepare the pesto, place the watercress and walnuts in a food processor and turn it on. Gradually add the olive oil until a thick paste forms and season with salt and black pepper.
· To prepare the salad, place the watercress in a bowl and toss with the walnut oil and vinegar. Season with salt and black pepper.
· To serve, place a tart on each plate and top with a handful of dressed watercress leaves and a dollop of pesto.

Wine expert Olly Smith's choice
Peter Lehmann Semillon

index

Entries in *italics* denote photographs.

acknowledgements

Amanda Ross, Executive Producer of *Saturday Kitchen* who devised and co-edited this book would like to thank the following for their considerable efforts:

Series Producer James Winter and the production team Dave Mynard, Elissa Standen and James Cook.
Will Learmonth for the screen grabs and original graphics.
Anna Ratcliffe for her endless eating (for the sake of the show of course) and proofing.
Janet Brinkworth and Helen Alexander-Gillen for food preparation.
Andy Clarke for his attitude and his washing up.
All our celebrity guests and the celebrity booking team, Charlotte Johnstone Jonathan Perry and Sinead Oldnall, who also wash up when we're pushed!
Director Dino Charalambous and the rest of the amazing happy crew (including Phil the Fork) who make getting up at 6 a.m. bearable.

The BBC Executives for all their support – Carla-Maria Lawson, Patricia Grey and Emma Swain.

And of course most of all James Martin, and all the amazing chefs and wonderful wine experts – it's a great privilege and an even greater pleasure working with you all!

10 9 8 7 6

Published in 2008 by BBC Books, an imprint of Ebury Publishing. A Random House Group Company

Copyright © Cactus TV 2008

Photography (full-page pictures) by Wil Heap, © Woodlands Book Limited 2008

The authors have asserted their right to be identified as the author of this Work in accordance with the Copyright, Designs and Patents Act 1988.

All rights reserved. No part of this publication may be reproduced, stored in a retrieval system, or transmitted in any form or by any means, electronic, mechanical, photocopying, recording or otherwise, without the prior permission of the copyright owner.

The Random House Group Limited Reg. No. 954009

Addresses for companies within the Random House Group can be found at www.randomhouse.co.uk
A CIP catalogue record for this book is available from the British Library.

ISBN 978 1 846 07283 3

The Random House Group Limited supports The Forest Stewardship Council (FSC), the leading international forest certification organisation. All our titles that are printed on Greenpeace approved FSC certified paper carry the FSC logo. Our paper procurement policy can be found at www.rbooks.co.uk/environment

Editor: Eleanor Maxfield
Copy-editor: Juliana Foster
Designer: Grade Design Limited
Home Economist: Janet Brinkworth
Colour origination by: Dot Gradations Ltd, UK
Printed and bound in Great Britain by Butler Tanner & Dennis Ltd, Frome, Somerset